Once Saved, Then What?

VERVELY JORDAN

Once Saved, Then What?
Copyright © 2021 by Vervely Jordan.

All rights reserved. No part of this book may be reproduced in any form or by any electronic or mechanical means, including information storage and retrieval systems, without permission in writing from the publisher and author, except by reviewers, who may quote brief passages in a review.

This publication contains the opinions and ideas of its author. It is intended to provide helpful and informative material on the subjects addressed in the publication. The author and publisher specifically disclaim all responsibility for any liability, loss, or risk, personal or otherwise, which is incurred as a consequence, directly or indirectly, of the use and application of any of the contents of this book.

ISBN: 978-1-63950-027-7   [Paperback Edition]
          978-1-63950-028-4   [eBook Edition]

Printed and bound in The United States of America.

Gateway Towards Success

8063 MADISON AVE #1252
Indianapolis, IN 46227

+13176596889
www.writersapex.com

I dedicate this to the loving memory of my five brothers and two sisters who have transitioned over, and especially to my parents, Rev. Mack and Velma Jordan, who planted the seed for Christianity in my life. I also dedicate this book to my husband Garry Williams and my remaining siblings Jearleana Parker, Larry (Janice) Jordan and Arvy (Linda) Jordan. I am so blessed that I had parents who were believers and who loved the Lord. They loved and cherished me all while they lived. For them, I truly thank God. One day, I shall see them again.

Contents

Preface..7
Prologue..9
Introduction..13
Chapter 1: What Is Salvation?...17
               Change: Does Salvation Bring About a Change? 22
               How Does Change Occur?.................................23
               Faith: What Is It?..24
               Communication..28
Chapter 2: Spiritual Growth (A Process) 32
               A Babe in Christ...34
               Young Adult in Christ 38
               Maturity in Christ...42
               Assurance of the Resurrection...........................45
Chapter 3: Babe's Stage of Spiritual Growth....................46
               A Babe in Christ:
                  More about Being a Babe in Christ 47
               Study the Word of God 51
Chapter 4: Young Adult Stage of Spiritual Growth..........57
               Spiritual Gifts...59
               One Body with Many Members 60
               Encounter with the Holy Spirit 68
               The Relationship...70
               Reading..73
               Peace 74
Chapter 5: An Effort Toward Maturity in Spiritual Growth 76
               Things I Do Not Do as I Should......................79
               Life's Journey..83
               My Personal Steps 86
               Personal Prayer Story..91
               The Armor of God 95
               Prayer...98
Conclusion...99
Reference...101

PREFACE

Would you believe that a person can grow up in a Christian home and know Jesus Christ all of their life and yet not truly know Jesus? You know that you have salvation and that Jesus Christ is your Lord and Savior. But with your life, you are asking yourself, *what am I to do*? Well, I am such a person.

I truly do not have answers, but I believe there are others who may have some of the same questions I have/had over the years. Some of you may have answers, but there are some of us who are prone to wonder all the time, seeking for something or for more knowledge about God. I have criticized myself so many times when I asked God a question; and in seeking the answer, I compare myself to someone else to say if I was more like them. I would have my answers or know your response, Lord, *wrong*. I continue to do it even though God tells me over and over not to compare myself because if he wanted me to be like them, *he* would have made me them.

The following are the thoughts of a confused Christian believing to be a saved person. I want to express thoughts that may help someone who may be confused as I had been about some of these religious issues, so you can know you are not alone. There is so much information presented that, without caution and discernment, it becomes very confusing. And to write it out helps me understand. The intention of this writing is not for direction or instructions. Its purpose is to assist in understanding an answer to a question in my mind.

The answer may be simple to some that you are to bring others to Christ, share your testimonies, and study God's Word—the Bible. But for me, I knew that. But that was not enough for my understanding. It could not be that simple, not for me.

PROLOGUE

The particular title of this book was given to me many years ago. I remember driving to work going to the Argonne National Laboratory in Argonne, Illinois, where I worked as an auditor for the United States of America Department of Energy. I lived in Matteson, Illinois. And on the way to work, I drove through the forest preserve, the scenic route.

Each morning as I drive to work, I would listen to different ministers on the radio or cassette tapes I purchased. I was listening to so much information that I was beginning to get confused because there was so many messages that instruct people how to live the Christian life. I was wondering because of my life and if I had a chance to get to heaven. I was feeling there was no way I could do all that was required. And during this time, I was trying to function with information overload.

One morning as I was praying on my way to work, the question came to me, "Once saved, then what?" And I have always believed that it was the Holy Spirit speaking to me and said, "There are many people who have the same question. And just maybe as you try to figure it out, write about it and share with others." Therefore, I decided to do just that.

I started writing to see if I could help myself. Once I got started, I thought at first I knew the answer, but with so much information available, I needed to clarify a few things. The straight answer was at the point you are saved. You then start to live a Christ-like life. As simple as that statement, it can cause many, many, many concerns.

I started to write a little and just a little over the years; but I began to think, why in the world would I believe I had anything to write about? I pushed it to the back burner of my mind and just went on with my confused life. I would remember the words ever so often, but then I pushed them back and moved on because I just could not believe I really had anything to say.

It now had been over twenty years, and I was thinking about trying to finish what I started. As I sat here, I asked the Lord to give me words, guidance, and strength to accomplish something that will help me and someone else.

I do believe that the focus of this book is to help beginning Christians. And by that, I do not mean *new*. I mean someone who knows he or she is saved, but so much information can get confusing without time to absorb and understand what you are hearing or reading. We all learn at different speed, levels, and ways so as the scriptures say in 2 Corinthians 10:12 which tells us "not to compare ourselves with others."

I do this so often. Each time I pray and ask God for help, in his quiet voice, he says, "Remember you are who I made you to be and stop comparing yourself with others."

I know I am hardheaded, and it takes longer for things to sink in. Just recently, I was driving along and thinking about something someone had told me. And I started asking, "Why not me, Lord?" And it was as if it was so clear that the Lord said, "How many times will I have to tell you to not compare yourself to others and concentrate on who I made you to be?"

I want so to finish this book, but I keep hitting roadblocks mostly of my own making. I think about this book a lot. Then I may be in a Sunday school class or just a study group, and I have discussions and various responses and think to myself. There is nothing I could possible say that has not already been said before.

Today as I sit here, my Father God says to me, "It may have been said before a million time, but the message may not have gotten to whom it should and will not, unless you do as I say and follow through with this assignment that you have been given."

I believe God gave me the title for a reason, and I searched the internet. It has not been used, so it is time I get off my duff and proceed. And my prayer is as follows:

Father God in heaven and in the name of Jesus, please guide my hands, thoughts, words, and actions to do what you have for me to do. I believe with all of my heart that you gave this message to me, and I want to share as you have me to. Thanks to you, Father God, for all you have done. And I ask your blessing on this message *book* to accomplish your will. Please move me out of the way, and let the Holy Spirit take control and guide me through the necessary processes to accomplish your will for my life with specific focus on this writing task. I thank you now in your precious Son named Jesus. *Amen.*

With that prayer said, I believe that I will be able to finally follow through with what I have to do. I had a conformation about this one recent Sunday while I was in church. This particular Sunday, my pastor (Dr. George Black, Rejoice Church, Olive Branch, MS) had prepared notes to preach from, but he said the Holy Spirit was sending him to a different direction. And with that, he focuses on the question.

If there is anything—place, person, or whatever—not to suggest too many things and put ideas on a person's mind, he said that God is saying it is time to do it. If it is to go, it's time to go. While he was talking, my mind centered on the book, the message, and that title I had been given. I truly believed that at this point, I was being told to buckle down and follow through with the task I had been given. By the grace of God and guidance of the Holy Spirit, I will accomplish my task.

Introduction

Trees in the backyard.

I am a Christian believer. In that statement, I mean I have accepted the Lord Jesus Christ as my Lord and Savior, and I believe that he arose from the dead to save me from condemnation. Furthermore, church involvement has been a major part of my life. I accepted the Lord Jesus Christ as my Lord and Savior at an early age and was baptized approximately at the age of twelve. I had never really departed from my belief in Jesus Christ, but I have not led a life of exemplary actions.

VERVELY JORDAN

My father, Rev. Mack Jordan, was a Southern Baptist minister. He ensured that I had knowledge of who Jesus Christ is and have him (Jesus) in my life. My father had at least two small churches at any single time. I followed him to his churches when I was very young. However, when I became active in my local church, I stayed home to remain active. I believe my parents raised all of their children to have morals and standards based on the Word of God (Bible). With a religious background I sometimes got a little confused. (But I always knew wrong from right.) I had such a mental struggle in my life sometime in trying to understand the ins and outs of it all. I heard during my life it is not hard. You simply have to know God, and he will guide you. But how do you simply know? I have known the truth (spiritual truth) for many years. But at times, I wonder what the purpose is. I pray, and I know the Lord hears me. He has answered many prayers, and I have known his answers of yes, no, and wait.

Growing up in a minister's household, I do not have the testimony of saved from some disastrous background such as drugs or abusive parents, etc. However, I should have no excuse for not being a steadfast believer. However, I have not been. I can say I truly thank God for my parents, and they were the initiators who wanted their children (eleven of us) to know Jesus Christ. They brought us up in the way we should go knowing we all have a will of our own.

For whatever I have done in my life, I cannot and will not blame my parents. I have a will, and what I've chosen to do or have done is of my own doing. I know, and I feel bless that I had good training growing up from my parents and our small neighborhood called Lakeview, Arkansas, about twelve miles south of Helena, Arkansas, that was right on the Mississippi River.

I have not been a monster or anything of the kind, but I have not had a focused concentrated life totally on Jesus Christ to make him the center and the reason for my being. As we Christians stress salvation, to nonbelievers, there could be that lingering quote in their minds, "Once saved, then what?" Is there more to this thing called salvation?

Before I get too deep, let me share a little more of my background. During my professional career, I moved around the United

States, and I have always found a church to attend to. When I was not attending church services with other believers, I could sense something was missing from my life. In reality, I knew when I was not associating with believers that something is missing. In April 1995, I moved to the Chicago, Illinois, area where I had lived before. I did not rush to find a church. I attended the previous church, but God did not touch my heart to reunite. I visited different churches and listened to religious radio and TV program. My desire to be involved in a church had diminished, and I was wondering why; but I had hunger for the Word. Confusion, *yes*. I listen to minister on the radio and television, and they talked a lot about salvation. They talked a lot about being lost and our need to accept Jesus Christ as our Savior. This truth I had accepted.

As I generally would do, I found a church where I got active participating doing just a little something. I have always believed I was to be of service in my local church. Well, one day as I previously stated, I was driving alone on my way home from work. A phrase came to me as I was listening to a religious tape. The phrase was "once saved, then what?" It was like I was missing something in my life, and I did not know that. I have salvation, but what could be missing?

However, I did not decide to do anything about it at the time. I just realized then that I had a deep concern about myself and religion. Sometime later, approximately a month or two, the same phrase came to mind again as I was driving home. Again, I did nothing. I just acknowledged the thought that maybe I should do something about it. But as I continue to drive, I forgot all about it.

Now for the third time, a few weeks later, it came to mind again. This time, I immediately got a pen and paper and jotted the phrase down while I was driving (not a good idea, I know), but I waited for the very next stoplight. I wrote the phrase down in my planner knowing that sometime later, I would probably come across it again.

Truly, it was some time later. I do not remember how long it was, but when I did see the phrase in my planner, I started to ponder on the subject. What is the answer, do you know? Can you ask someone or search it out yourself? Is there a simple answer or not? At this point, I decided I would get my Bible's reference materials and search for an answer to my question "then what?" I really wanted a summary answer in hope that I could clear up this struggle I had in my mind. I had many answers in my mind, but none were sufficient to clearly answer my question.

As I work through this, I prayed and asked the Lord for guidance. And I do wonder if there really is a simple answer or is the Christian life the "then what?" It is my hope and desire to learn as I search for an answer. This may sound like a simple question, but in some of our minds, it is not that simple. There are structured answers I know and have heard all my life. But a real, clear, understandable answer is the one I am searching for that makes this clear as a bell ringing in my ear on my own mind.

The first step to understanding my problem, I thought, would be to research the biblical definition of salvation and any other explanations of salvation that I could find. Well, it is time to go and see what this journey finds. I know I will learn something along the way.

I believe there are so many things that could be explained more to simplify a believer's belief. I sometimes think I am not giving people enough credit. Then I hear the Holy Spirit say to me, "You were given a task to do, and you should do it and not try to rationalize the results because the Father has told you what to do. And do not make any reference to what people already know because this message is for some special people whom you have no idea of who they are. Just follow your leadings and do as you have been guided to do."

CHAPTER 1

What Is Salvation?

My hometown lake "Old Town Lake," Lakeview, Arkansas

On occasions, as a believer, when I would speak about salvation and being saved, I was asked, "Saved from what?" With that said, if you ask that question, this information is for you. Starting with the hasting dictionary of the Bible, the definition of salvation refers to "the generic term employed in Scripture to express the idea of any gracious deliverance of God, but specially of the Spiritual redemption from sin and its consequences predicted by the Old Testament prophets and realized in the mission and work of the Savior Jesus Christ."

To express my layperson understanding of salvation would be to say "not being separated from God." Salvation is knowing that I have an eternal place with my Father who art in heaven and to know that there is only one way to get there as recorded in Scripture. And that is believing in the death burial and resurrection of Jesus Christ.

In scripture John 3:16 (NIV), it says, "For God so loved the world that he gave his one and only Son, that whoever believes in him shall not perish but have eternal life."

Another version express as follows, "For God so loved the world that he gave his only Son, so that everyone who believes in him may not perish but may have eternal life" (John 3:16, NRSV).

If I were to simplify it, I would say God saved us from ourselves by allowing his Son to die for us. To some people, if you are at least in your fifties, you may remember years ago that the aforementioned scripture John 3:16 would be posted on signs and held up at football games.

During those years, the cameras would always show the signs. One Monday morning, after a Sunday afternoon football game, one of my coworkers asked me, "What was John 3:16?"

I quoted it and explained that it was a scripture from the Bible. The next question was, what does that mean? I learned the meaning at an early age because my parents took me to Sunday school and church services. For this adult coworker to ask me that question, I began to understand or, should I say, realize that there are many people out there living a condemned life and do not know it.

However, when I think of my salvation, I feel comfort in knowing that I will have eternal life with my God. I feel sad when I think about all the people who were and even now not taught about God, never been to church, never read the Bible, and are living a life not knowing that by God's grace, Jesus died on the cross so that they could, through faith, spend eternity with him in heaven. I have comfort knowing that to spend eternity with God is wonderful.

What more could a person want? I found that a good question, but my focus is to those who do not know nor have heard what is available. It hurts when I realize that so many people are missing out because they do not know how to trust that Jesus is Lord and that we can talk directly to him. God hears prayers, and *God* is real.

I will be continuing with the definition of *salvation* according to the Webster dictionary. It defines *salvation* as (1) a saving or being saved from danger, evil, difficult, destruction, etc. rescue; (2) a person or thing that is a means, cause, or source of preservation or rescue; and (3) the deliverance from sin and from the penalties of sin; redemption.

Redemption, according to Webster, (1) is a buying back, in release from sin; (2) a redeeming or being redeemed; and (3) something that redeems.

Because of the sacrifice of Jesus Christ, we have been redeemed. He bought us back from sin. Prior to being redeemed, mankind lived under the law. God gave the Ten Commandments to show mankind how lost/disconnected mankind was from him. Under the law were the strict rules mankind needed for instruction. Without guidance and instructions, we are all lost from knowing how God intended for mankind to live. When I think about God giving the law, I imagine the people were wondering around with no direction, and the Bible talks about this. But for my purpose, I do not need to discuss mankind wondering, and I will not discuss that. However, God had to provide instructions to mankind, so he gave us the law. I read and reread Romans 7:7–13 (MSG) to help my understanding of the deep need for the law. The writer of Romans expressed it as follows:

> But I can hear you say, "If the law code was as bad as all that, it's no better than sin itself." That's certainly not true. The law code had a perfectly legitimate function. Without its clear guidelines for right and wrong, moral behavior would be mostly guesswork. Apart from the succinct, surgical command, "You shall not covet," I could have dressed covetousness up to look like a virtue and ruined my life with it.

> Don't you remember how it was? I do, perfectly well. The law code started out as an excellent piece of work. What happened, though, was that sin found a way to pervert the command into a temptation, making a piece of "forbidden fruit" out of it. The law code, instead of being used to guide me, was used to seduce me. Without all the paraphernalia of the law code, sin looked pretty dull and lifeless, and I went along without paying much attention to it. But once sin got its hands on the law code and decked itself out in all that finery, I was fooled, and fell for it. The very command that was supposed to guide me into life was cleverly used to trip me up, throwing me headlong. So sin was plenty alive, and I was stone dead. But the law code itself is God's good and common sense, each command sane and holy counsel.
>
> I can already hear your next question: "Does that mean I can't even trust what is good [that is, the law]? Is good just as dangerous as evil?" No again! Sin simply did what sin is so famous for doing: using the good as a cover to tempt me to do what would finally destroy me. By hiding within God's good commandment, sin did far more mischief than it could ever have accomplished on its own. (Romans 7:7–13, MSG)

Jesus Christ bought us back from sin—we have been redeemed. Therefore, it is up to each individual to make our own choice. The writer in Colossians tells us that Jesus Christ sacrifice was for us all, and we have to believe and follow him. According to Scriptures, Colossians 2:14–15 (NIV) says:

> Having canceled the charge of our legal indebtedness, which stood against us and con-

demned us; he has taken it away, nailing it to the cross. And having disarmed the powers and authorities, he made a public spectacle of them, triumphing over them by the cross.

For mankind to have the opportunity to be saved was at a very high price. This does not mean that the law is not still valid because it is valid as it remains in the Scriptures. The writer in Romans tells us about the price that Jesus paid for us and did not have to; but because of love, he chose to, as stated in the following scripture.

> So, my friends, this is something like what has taken place with you. When Christ died he took that entire rule-dominated way of life down with him and left it in the tomb, leaving you free to "marry" a resurrection life and bear "offspring" of faith for God. For as long as we lived that old way of life, doing whatever we felt we could get away with, sin was calling most of the shots as the old law code hemmed us in. And this made us all the more rebellious. In the end, all we had to show for it was miscarriages and stillbirths. But now that we're no longer shackled to that domineering mate of sin, and out from under all those oppressive regulations and fine print, we're free to live a new life in the freedom of God. (Romans 7:4–6, MSG)

I, as a believer, understanding what Jesus has done for me and gratefully accept my salvation, and, to repeat myself on purpose, God loves us. I know nothing I say is valid unless I include scriptures to back it up, and I will do just that. Scripture tells us the need to be saved and by whom this option was provided.

"For God sent not his Son into the world to condemn the word; but that the world through him might be saved" (John 3:17, KJV).

VERVELY JORDAN

Change: Does Salvation Bring About a Change?

Does mankind change because of salvation? I thought so and still do according to Scripture.

> So if anyone is in Christ, there is a new creation; everything old has passed away, see, everything become new! All this is from God, who reconciled us to himself through Christ, and has given us the ministry of reconciliation; that is, in Christ God was reconciling the world to himself, not counting their trespasses against them, and entrusting the message of reconciliation to us. (2 Corinthians 5:17–19, NRSV)

To understand the possible change, let's look at our structure our makeup design. We were made in the image of *God*. We have a human body where our spiritual side resides. A new believer sometimes starts out on a spiritual and emotional high not knowing it will not last forever, and generally, when the emotional high is gone, so is the interest.

When I ask the question "then what?" I am not referring to a new believer because for a new believer, I clearly understand what's next; and that is to want to know Jesus Christ. For them, what is it for someone who has lost that emotional high and begins to doubt the reasons for it all, asking questions such as "what's the point?" because we want to maintain that emotional high and wonder if it is more than attending church services and going home with hopes that your life will be fine.

Then what is it all about?

It is all about salvation and a relationship. Salvation is a choice that each person has to make for themselves. And from all the scriptures I have used so far, they express it certainly that it is a gift to us from *God*. It is truly our choice to accept it or deny it. We can no way earn our salvation. It is a gift from God.

Since this is a gift, there is nothing for us to do, right? Wrong! You can be offered a gift, but until you receive it, it is not yours. I cannot express it enough. Salvation is a gift from *God*, and by God's grace and love, we have the option to be saved and be reconciled with our Father in heaven. Take your gift, received your gift, and be changed. By not accepting this free gift, you would be condemning yourself to eternal separation from *God*—the *God* who made you and who loves you.

How Does Change Occur?

There can be no change unless we have a change in our mind. The way we think dictates how and who we are. I heard once that if you keep thinking the way you think and get the same results that you do not like, then you need to change your thinking.

According to Romans 12:2 (NIV), it states: "Do not conform to the pattern of this world, but be transformed by the renewing of your mind. Then you will be able to test and approve what God's will is—his good, pleasing and perfect will."

However, there is the symbolic change in our lives when we are baptized as John the Baptist baptized the ones who came to him as described in Matthew 3:11–12 (NIV) as follows: "I baptize you with water for repentance, but one who is more powerful than I is coming after me; I am not worthy to carry his sandals."

In Matthew 21:32 (TLB), it also says, "For John the Baptist told you to *repent* and turn to God, and you wouldn't, while very evil men and prostitutes did. And even when you saw this happening, you refused to *repent*, and so you couldn't believe."

What John was describing is the water of baptism that is our public testament that one has accepted Jesus Christ as his/her savior. This act represents the death, burial, and resurrection of Christ because we go down in the water (death) burying our past sins forever and rising to a clean new life starting out repenting and believing and having a new slate to experience no condemnation for future sins.

A noticeable change occurs through knowledge and the baptism of the Holy Spirit. The more you know about God the Father, the Son, and the Holy Spirit, the more we change. Do not think as I once did, thinking that once I was saved, there was going to be some immediate gratification or supernatural change in my thinking to prove to myself I was saved. But when I did not see this type change in my life, I wondered about my salvation. At this point, I had to question myself and step back to ask myself, where is my faith? Our real thinking change comes with knowledge. Because of knowledge, *I* remembered what Jesus said in the scripture John 20:27–29 (NIV).

> Then he said to Thomas, "Put your finger here; see my hands. Reach out your hand and put it into my side. Stop doubting and believe." Thomas said to him, "My Lord and my God!"
> Then Jesus told him, "Because you have seen me, you have believed; blessed are those who have not seen and yet have believed."

I am truly blessed because Jesus said I was blessed because I believed and had not seen. To my surprise, there was no super natural change. But there is a heart change, and other people may notice this change in you before you do. When we have both the mind and heart change, this is the real change. You feel, and others see.

I just mentioned that I questioned my faith, so I want to talk a little about faith.

Faith: What Is It?

Hebrews 11:1–3 (NKJV) says that by faith, we understand.

> Now faith is the substance of things hoped for, the evidence of things not seen. For by it the elders obtained a good testimony.
> By faith we understand that the worlds were framed by the word of God, so that the things which are seen were not made of things which are visible.

There is no better definition of faith than this. I do not need Webster or anything else but God's Word for this definition.

A new believer is to want to get to know more about this person we believe in and to share with other that Jesus is the only way to God the Father with whom we expect to spend eternity. We have to believe what the Bible says and desire to study his Word.

However, at several different points or stages in my life, I began to feel a little overwhelmed knowing certain things and knowing God does not need my help, but I have a purpose. Maybe I am not giving myself credit for understanding because I know if we plant the seed in the mind of a person, it is truly God who makes the increase and provides the understanding. So just maybe I should look at my task as the planter of the seed that God has given me. I also know that what we sow has to be harvested, therefore, be careful what we sow because seeds of hate will reap hate; so try to sow seeds of love and reap love that pleases God.

Salvation can appear to be simple, and it is believing and receiving God's grace and having faith. Therefore, I am saved. However, Christians' obligations do not stop there. That is what I am learning to express. That supernatural change I was looking for did not happen. I have learned that when we are saved, there is a change; but not one that is visible to the naked eye per say.

As we are described to be made in the image of God; therefore, we are a body, a spirit, and a soul. I like the way it was described to me recently that we are a spirit living in a body with a soul. With that said, still I ask, "then what?" Here, I want to address the hope of a Christian our salvation. We have a hope of being with our Lord in heaven with a new body someday. As described in scripture 2 Corinthians 5:1–7 (NIV), it says:

> For we know that if the earthly tent we live in is destroyed, we have a building from God, an eternal house in heaven, not build by human hands. Meanwhile we groan, longing to be clothed instead with our heavenly dwelling because when we are clothed, we will not be found naked.

> For while we are in this tent, we groan and are burdened, because we do not wish to be unclothed but to be clothed instead with our heavenly dwelling, so that what is mortal may be swallowed up by life. Now the one who has fashioned us for this very purpose is God, who has given us the Spirit as a deposit, guaranteeing what is to come. Therefore we are always confident and know that as long as we are at home in the body we are away from the Lord. For we live by faith, not by sight.

Also according to 2 Timothy 2:15 (NIV), we are to "study to show thyself approved unto God, a workman that needeth not to be ashamed, rightly dividing the word of truth."

The King James Version says it this way, "Do your best to present yourself to God as one approved by him, a worker who has no need to be ashamed rightly explaining the word of truth" (II Timothy 2:15, KJV).

Although we cannot earn salvation from works, we should study God's Word; and his light will shine through us by the Holy Spirit and our knowledge. God wants you to come to him just as you are. Give *him* your life and believe on his Son, Jesus Christ. I believe that God is always there for us, but he will not go against our will because he gave us freewill. Having freewill means to me that we are free to do as we please, and he has opened the door for us to make our own choices. How can we be assured of our salvation? Well, once the Holy Spirit lives inside of you, as a Christian/believer, you have assurance of your salvation. And you know you are truly a child of God. The scriptures describe it as being a new person—born again.

However, God has fore knowledge of what we will do according to Roman 8:29–30 (KJV):

> And we know that all thing works together for good to them that love God, to them who are the called according to his purpose. For whom

> he did foreknow, he also did predestinate to be conformed to the image of his Son, that he might be the firstborn among many brethren. Moreover whom he did predestinate, them he also called: and who he called, them he also justified: and whom he justified, them he also glorified. What shall we then say to these things? If God be for us, who can be against us?

Another version I like is Romans 8:29–30 (TLB) below:

> And we know that all that happens to us is working for our good if we love God and are fitting into his plans. For from the very beginning God decided that those who came to him—and all along he knew who would—should become like his Son, so that his Son would be the First, with many brothers. And having chosen us, he called us to come to him; and when we came, he declared us "not guilty," filled us with Christ's goodness, gave us right standing with himself, and promised us his glory.

God is always waiting for us; and once we search for him, he is right there. God is not lost, we are. Accepting salvation appears easy, and it is believing and receiving. However, Christian's desires should not stop there which is my purpose for writing. By God's grace and faith on our part, we have salvation. My question "Then what?" is directed to a young adult who wants to mature. A more mature believer is one who has studied and knows something about the Scriptures and has experienced God's love and devotion and with whom God has answered prayers.

Then the question after salvation, "Then what?" is more than believing and accepting Jesus Christ as Lord and savior it includes growing spiritually to living a life like Christ. I have since learned there is a simple answer, and it is to live Christlike. But to do that, we have to know how Christ lived and who he is through reading and studying God's Words he provided for us.

Next let me talk a little about Christianity. I will use the words believer and Christian interchangeably as I discuss information based on my faith and what I particularly believe.

A Christian believer is one who believes that Jesus Christ is the Son of God and that he (Jesus) came to this earth and was hung on a cross and died thereby becoming our Lord and Savior. I believed that when we are truly saved, we automatically are believers. I can remember one time when I was home with my mother one Sunday afternoon. And often, we would discuss the Bible, or I would be asking questions. And this particular Sunday, I was reading the Bible; but I do not remember (the particular) scripture, but I was confused and was saying to my mother that it just did not make sense. And she said to me that my understanding of God's Word would become clear when God reveals it to me. She said, "Sometime, you are not meant to understand at that time. God will reveal his truth to you when it is your time, and to remember it is all in God's timing."

I continued to read and ask questions. And I have to say over the years, it has been as she said. Some things I understand now were simply just word calling years ago. I am a believing Christian with faith in God, my Father, in heaven.

Communication

God, who is Spirit, communicates with our spirits according to Romans 8:9–11 (NRSV):

> But you are not in the flesh; you are in the Spirit, since the Spirit of God dwells in you. Anyone who does not have the Spirit of Christ does not belong to him. But if Christ is in you through the body is dead because of sin, the Spirit is life because of righteousness. If the Spirit of him who raised Jesus from the dead dwells in

> you, he who raised Christ from the dead will give life to your mortal bodies also through his Spirit that dwells in you.

As a believing Christian, I know the Holy Spirit is real, and I have learned to fix my mind to understand that the Holy Spirit is *God*.

In summary, just think if salvation is a gift. Now imagine it as if someone is giving you a brand-new automobile as a gift. The automobile is all yours, and you have to do nothing to get it. It was a gift because someone loved you just that much. Now that you have the automobile at no cost to you, it is truly yours to have forever. But how long it last depends on how you maintain it because the upkeep is all in your hands.

What we do with our salvation is all in our hands. I am saved from sin by grace, and I have a reserved place in heaven. And I can know this for sure. How about you?

If we are saved by the grace of God, then why should there be anything else for us to do? Jesus did it all, so why could there possibly be confusion? But it can be. I find the following scripture great for closing this chapter.

> Blessed is the man who does not walk in the counsel of the wicked or stand in the way of sinner or sit in the seat of mockers. But his delight is in the law of the Lord and on his law he meditates day and night. He is like a tree planted by streams of water, which yield its fruit in season and wither whatever he does prospers. Not so the wicked! They are like chaff that the wind blows away. Therefore the wicked will not stand in the judgment, nor sinners in the assembly of the righteous. For the Lord watches over the way of the righteous, but the way of the wicked will perish. (Psalms 1:1–6, NIV)

As usual, I like to compare versions. Below is Psalm 1:1–6 (TLB):

> Oh, the joys of those who do not follow evil men's advice, who do not hang around with sinners, scoffing at the things of God. But they delight in doing everything God wants them to, and day and night are always meditating on his laws and thinking about ways to follow him more closely.
>
> They are like trees along a riverbank bearing luscious fruit each season without fail. Their leaves shall never wither, and all they do shall prosper. But for sinners, what a different story! They blow away like chaff before the wind. They are not safe on Judgment Day; they shall not stand among the godly. For the Lord watches over all the plans and path of godly men, but the paths of the godless lead to doom.

Finally, I was taught something called the Romans Road which is a simplified guide to describe salvation. It is as follows first go to the Romans 3:23 (TLB),"Yes, all have sinned; all fall short of God's glorious ideal."

Then "For the wages of sin is death, but the free gift of God is eternal life through Jesus Christ Our Lord" (Romans 6:23, TLB).

Next Romans 5:8 (TLB) says, "But God showed his great love for us by sending Christ to die for us while we were still sinners."

Next Romans 10:9–10 (TLB) states:

> For if you tell others with your own mouth that Jesus Christ is your Lord, and believe in your own heart that God has raised him from the dead, you will be saved. For it is by believing in his heart that a man becomes right with God;

and with his mouth he tells others of his faith, confirming his salvation.

And finally, Romans 10:13 (TLB) states: "Anyone who calls upon the name of the Lord will be saved." The answer to my question is beginning to become clearer. I am beginning to get it—the "then what?" of it. To paraphrase, Ephesians 2:8 says that our salvation is a gracious gift from God. God chose us as his people out of his love for just us. Jesus then die to pay the penalty for our sin, and the Holy Spirit (through his blood) cleanses us from sin when we believe.

My preliminary answer to my "then what?" is that there are stages we have to go through. It is a growth process, and this process can be complicated. Therefore, I will discuss three stages in the following chapters.

- Ask yourself the flowing questions and give a truthful answer.
- What does salvation mean to you? Take time to write your answer.
- Who is Jesus to you?
- How important is what Jesus did for you?
- Are you saved? If not, what will be your next step?

Chapter 2

Spiritual Growth (A Process)

Niagara Falls

ONCE SAVED, THEN WHAT?

First, I will briefly describe the phases of growth that I call the three stages and provide more details later. Over the years, I have learned that the "then what?" has no such thing as a simple single answer. The "then what" is the beginning to your new life. However, this is where some of the most misunderstandings happened for me. I had a vision that when people talked about a changed life that I was actually going to change, it would be a letdown when I did not immediately make a complete personality change. I was not looking for a physical change. I was thinking that my mind and my way of thinking and feelings would be so different immediately. Little did I know that I did not know enough for my thinking to change. Praise to God that our spiritual life is not our physical life. We have so much to learn. This is the point I realized that I had a lot more growing to do and some people just grow faster than others.

I realized that the "then what?" as previously stated, is the growth process after salvation. It is all about a process. In this growth process, I have defined the three stages as follows: babe, young adult, and maturing adult. Regardless of stages, I do want to emphasize that the very first step is and always will be that free-gift salvation and on to the spiritual growth process. This is why Paul wrote in 1 Corinthians 3:1–2 (NIV) which states, "Brothers and sisters, I could not address you as people who live by the Spirit but as people who are still worldly—mere infants in Christ."

I also like the living Bible version 1 Corinthians 3:1–2:

> Dear brothers, I have been talking to you as though you were still just babies in the Christian life who are not following the Lord but your own desires; I cannot talk to you as I would to healthy Christians who are filled with the Spirit. I have had to feed you with milk and not with solid food because you couldn't digest anything stronger. And even now you still have to be fed on milk.

Praise God. It is a process, and we all progress at our own pace.

A Babe in Christ

Nigeria Falls

I do not think it can be said enough that the first step regardless of stage is salvation (our acceptance of Jesus Christ as our Lord and Savior). And at this point, regardless of physical age, we all are infants—a baby in Christ. This is our beginning immediately after being saved or *born again* in the Spirit as the Bible says. We are made in the image of God. Therefore, I have this body where my spirit and soul reside as explained in the following scripture.

> Flesh gives birth too flesh, but the Spirit gives birth to Spirit. You should not be surprised at my saying you must be born again. The wind blows wherever it pleases. You here its sound, but you cannot tell where it comes from or where it is going. So it is with everyone born of the Spirit. (John 3:6–8, NIV)

Our rebirth into believing is our spiritual birth, our pathway into the kingdom of God. In the scriptures, Jesus explained as he was teaching Nicodemus. Nicodemus, as the Bible described him, was a man who was one of the Pharisees. Being one of the Pharisees would mean that Nicodemus was a man of position. He was one of the rulers of the Jews. The Bible say Nicodemus looked at Jesus as a teacher sent from God, and Nicodemus was curious; and the Bible recorded a discussion between Jesus and Nicodemus as recorded in John 3:1–6 (KJV):

> There was a man of the Pharisees, named Nicodemus, a ruler of the Jews: The same came to Jesus by night, and said unto him, Rabbi, we know that thou art a teacher come from God: for no man can do these miracles that thou doest, except God be with him. Jesus answered and said unto him, "Verily, verily, I say unto thee, except a man be born again, he cannot see the Kingdom of God."
>
> Nicodemus saith unto him, "How can a man be born when he is old? Can he enter the second time into his mother's womb, and be born?"
>
> Jesus answered, "Verily, verily, I say unto thee, except a man be born of water and of the Spirit, he cannot enter into the Kingdom of God. That which is born of the flesh is flesh; and that which is born of the Spirit is spirit."

Another version is of John 3:1–6 (TLB) that says:

> After dark one night a Jewish religious leader named Nicodemus, a member of the sect of the Pharisees, came for an interview with Jesus. "Sir," he said, "we all know that God has sent you to teach us. Your miracles are proof enough of this."

> Jesus replied, "With all the earnestness I possess I tell you this unless you are born again, you can never get into the Kingdom of God"
>
> "Born again!" exclaimed Nicodemus. "What do you mean? How can an old man go back into his mother's womb and be born again?"
>
> Jesus replied, "What I am telling you so earnestly is this: Unless one is born of water and the Spirit, he cannot enter the Kingdom of God. Men can only reproduce human life, but the Holy Spirit gives new life from heaven."

Jesus tells us that our physical birth is not enough. You must be born spiritually. The spiritual birth is the birth of the Holy Spirit in us. The Holy Spirit is our communicator to *God*, our creator.

At times, when talking with people, I find that the discussion of being born again is so foreign, yet the Bible talk about it several times. For example, in 1 Peter 1:23, we find the following:

"For you have been born again, not of perishable seed, but of imperishable, through the living and enduring word of God" (1 Peter 1:23, NIV); and "For you have a new life. It was not passed on to you from your parents, for the life they gave you will fade away. This new one will last forever, for it comes from Christ, God's ever-living Message to men" (1 Peter 1:23, TLB).

We are saved from condemnation, saved from ourselves this broken human body, and had been given a spiritual rebirth being reconciled with our heavenly Father.

However, over the years, I have seen new baby Christians fall away too soon after the initial excitement. Sad because we lose some people during this baby stage sometimes because we teach (provide) meat when we should be teaching (providing) only milk. We can teach over the baby's head while the baby is excited and not yet understand the reason for the excitement. At this point, the baby is surviving on excitement and being fed with the wrong food that could cause damage in the spiritual life the same as giving meat to a baby when that little system is not ready.

The baby believer is first excited with great expectations and should enjoy it but at the same time learn that the excitement may fade, but know that this will not mean that your salvation is gone. When we skip the little messages, it, sometime, is not made clear.

For example, I was once in a Bible class on Wednesday night at a local church where I attended. And the classes were good. We were actually being taught using the Bible and studying by book. At the end of one of the classes, I talked to another student; and she said to me how much she liked the class, but the people in the class all knew and talked about characters from the Bible that she had never heard of in her previous religion. She said this makes her feel dumb and lost, at times, during the discussions, yet she wanted to learn. I told her I understood, but I was not sure how to help. I thought about myself and how I did not feel that I was one who could go to leadership and say anything; so it goes in a cycle, and no one got helped. As I think about it, I lost an opportunity to help someone who later moved on.

Considering theses stages, there is no set length of time to know how long each stage will last. This all depends on each individual because we are all made different by our creator who wanted it that way. Trust and believe that you are who God made you to be.

If you are reading this and are a new believer, I want to express to you to not feel bad. Ask questions when you do not understand. No one knows it all. Please understand that the excitement may fade, and if or when it does, you are truly okay. Express your concerns, and if there is no one in that place to help, try somewhere else, but pray first asking God for guidance to lead you to where he wants you to be. By all that is within you, never, never give up. Ask the Father in heaven, and he will help you. Be patient because God is always busy doing for his children. You are saved now, and you are an heir according to Romans 8:17 as follows:

> And if children, then heirs of God, and joint—heirs with Christ, if so be that we suffer with him, if we may be also glorified together. And since we are his children, we will share his

treasures—for all God gives to his Son Jesus is now ours too. But if we are to share his glory, we must also share his suffering.

Young Adult in Christ

Old Town Lake, Lake View, Arkansas

The second stage of development if we continue to grow, and the keyword here is grow. And the other is we have to make a conscious effort to grow. This is not by any means of an automatic process. I call this the *young adult stage*. For me, this was the most frustrating and confusing stage of my spiritual growth process. At this point, I thought I knew all I needed to know. But in reality, I did not. This is much the same in our human growth process. Therefore, the name reference relates as before babe's now young adults. There are the teen years, but I am not addressing that group because being a teen has a ton of issues on its own, and one is truly not old enough to know and too old not to. With no training, just a lost group, and so it is with our teens and their spiritual growth life without leadership.

It hurts knowing that there is such a lost generation because they had no training and particularly no praying parents.

So as I talk about maturity, I believe in our lifetime our spiritual growth process will never reach completion. We continue to grow until we are called home where our spiritual life lasts forever as stated in 1 Peter 1:23 (TLB) as shown on page 36.

I also find this to be a very interesting stage because I had grown enough to know some things, but my approach to understanding was wrong, and I believe I knew more than I really do, it caused me to sometimes single out people and make judgments believing I knew enough to condemn someone because of their actions. And when we do things like this, I found that we open the door for possible destruction of another person's hope and can potentially stunt any chance of growth in another person.

This is why I know we have spiritual growth stages to go through just as there are stages we must go through in our daily human physical lives. We cannot go from infancy to adulthood without chronologically reaching what the world calls legal adult age of twenty-one. Even at the world's adult age of twenty-one, some people take much longer to really become a responsible adult. Sad to say that some never seem to grow up. Regardless of age, there is always more to learn. However, at this stage, we have learned and know for a fact that we are saved.

Our salvation is no longer in question. We can start looking forward to a rewarding life in heaven spending eternity with our creator. However, at this stage, the last thing a lot of young people think about is leaving this earth. At that point, the young person (like I was) is looking forward to a long and (in our minds) a never-ending life. The world has so many distractions that during this time, it becomes so easy to fall away from the real meaning of being a believer. If anyone reading this was like me, I was thinking that I had plenty of time never thinking how it could be cut short. The world opens so many doors, and as a young adult, we foolishly try to enter them all. This is where I have to thank my Father in heaven for praying parents who kept me prayed up. Because of many foolish actions, things could have happened to me and completely destroyed my life.

For example, I remember while I was living in Northern Virginia, Centreville, Virginia, I had a little sports car, a five-speed automatic Acura. I learned to drive using a standard transmission and always enjoyed driving one most of my life. Well, this particular day after work, when I was dropped off at the park and ride lot, I got into my car and proceeded to the first stoplight. It is a dead-end street, and you can only go either right or left. Right was home, but I had decided to make the left and do a little shopping. As I sat there at the light, I was in a good mood thinking that when that light turns green, I am going to give this little car all its got and burn rubber as I make this turn. Well, folks, the light changed to green. And I hit the gas, but my car did not move. And at that exact moment, a car coming through the intersection ran the light. If my car had moved, that would have been an awful accident. I know how to drive my car meaning to take off as I planned. I know I had to have my car in first gear, and as I looked down, I saw that my car was not in any gear.

I never sit at a light without having my car in first gear for a smooth take off. I could not wait to get home and call my mother to tell her what had happened. Someone may say that I was a lucky person, but I would think not. I was a blessed person. Oddly enough, a few weeks earlier, I had just finished reading a book on how God uses angels, and I started to think how wonderful it is if just maybe we do have a guardian angel watching over us with God's instructions. I just think it could have been my angle who changed my gear. (Smile. God is good). This is just one example of how careless we can behave, and when we are protected, we should always give thanks to God for being there.

No one nor I have found in the Word that it says living a believer's life would be easy, and it is not. But our enemy is out there prowling around on every street and looking at every place to devour us. One thing I know for sure as the Bible says, "Train up a child in the way he should go. There is a good chance we will not be lost." However, we may backslide/depart; but because of that grounded training, we will only go so far. And some of us find our way back, and I do believe others are taken home early, why, I do not know. I just know our Father God protests his children.

It is during this stage where I found myself straddle the fence—I had God and believing on one side, but I had the world and partying on the other side trying to enjoy both worlds without consequences. All the time, I was doing my own thing with no real regard for God. I could hear that little voice deep inside condemning me, but I pushed it back and kept going. And because I never fully deserted the church, that voice got louder and louder until I heard what he was saying, and it was time to make a change. I knew in my heart I could do better and put more focus on God, and I began to learn to start and take a few small steps at a time to learn more and more about who I called my Lord and my Savior.

I realize this is just my opinion. However, during this phase, it is when more often the growth process becomes stagnant. We go to church services on Sunday mornings only as an attender (benchwarmer) not participating. I did this for years, then I move up to attending some special classes that were offered, especially when there was Sunday school which is not so popular anymore. But it was great for getting to know people and getting a bit closer to God's Word especially for me because I moved around a lot. As a working person, I found it so hard to do anything outside of Sunday services. Because my job required a lot of travel, I basically never got into midweek services.

While at St. Marks, a local church I attended in Illinois, I actually looked forward to Tuesday night Bible study with friends and family. At this particular church, the Bible study consisted of actual Bible study. The pastor would have someone read the scriptures and tell them when to start and stop, and he would explain/discuss the actual scriptures. This was the largest Bible class I had ever experienced. It was in the sanctuary, and there were always at least forty to fifty people in attendance. We all had our Bibles and read along. And, of course, we could ask questions.

I enjoyed this so very much. And wouldn't you know it just as I was beginning to enjoy the lessons I actually got the promotion on my job I had applied for and moved to Northern Virginia. Once I moved and started looking for another church, I found myself looking for more than just another church. I had a need to learn more, so

I thought about Bible College, but with my job and travel this would not work. Therefore, I started to look for other Bible training, and I found where this particular church Capital Baptist had (Capital Baptist Institute, Annandale, Virginia) established by Rev Steve Reynolds was offering evening classes with a curriculum leading to a diploma in Bible studies. I signed up and started classes. I really felt like I was learning and enjoyed my lessons. It was a three-year course. Yeah, I finished. This may not work for some people, but it is what I found I needed.

Through this Bible school, I started attending the church. And I found this church had Sunday school and the material used and openness of the classes and the variety of classes such as married, single, female, men, and couples. There was a class for everyone. I attended the women-only class. From this school, I felt I was at a point to reach for maturity which is what I call my third stage.

Maturity in Christ

Colorado

This is where I would place seasoned Christians—ones who have learned much about God and know how to handle things and the one we go to for directions and guidance. Although I called this stage mature, we never grow up because our mind could never hold all that God has. Maturity is a stage of growth where you should have gotten closer to God and look more to the day when we will see Jesus face-to-face. It's not that I am saying we are getting ready to die, but our relationship at this point is closer, and we better understand our relationship with God.

As for me, I am so far from being a mature Christian. It is scary realizing how much I do not know. Each time I listen to good messages, I learn something, and this continue to open my mind to how much there is to know and believe no one really reaches maturity. We just keep running our race until it is over. When I say over, I mean we have finished the race as Paul quoted in scripture 2 Timothy 4:7-8 and Philippians 3:12-15.

> I have fought the good fight, I have finished the race, I have kept the faith. Finally, there is laid up for me the crown of righteousness, which the Lord, the righteous Judge, will give to me on that Day, and not to me only but also to all who have loved His appearing. (2 Timothy 4:7–8, NKJV)

Pressing toward the goal:

> Not that I have already attained, or am already perfected; but I press on, that I may lay hold of that for which Christ Jesus has also laid hold of me. Brethren, I do not count myself to have apprehended; but one thing I do, forgetting those things which are behind and reaching forward to those things which are ahead, I press toward the goal for the prize of the upward call of God in Christ Jesus.
> Therefore let us, as many as are mature, have this mind; and if in anything you think otherwise, God will reveal even this to you. (Philippians 3:12–15, NKJV)

At this point, we have learned how to ask, pray, and learn more about what God has for you to do and just do it. He will give you the desire and ability to accomplish what he has for you to do like Paul, so we can finish our race.

I prayed and asked God in the name of Jesus to allow the Holy Spirit to direct my thinking and writing to present the information in an understanding form for others and myself. And as I proceed, I have to believe my prayer is being answered. As you may notice, I do not have long prayers, but I do have many.

I am sure you will be just as I am realizing as we grow and live. We will keep running into obstacles, but this is when I have/had to rely on my faith and trust that I am doing what I am assigned to do. For me, this particular assignment has taken at least forty years for me to get to this point. I say forty years because the first twenty years, I spent wondering and looking. I hope that if when someone reads this, it will help them cut those wondering years short maybe. As I look back, since I am discussing maturity, if I had tried to write this twenty years ago, I would not have known what I know now nor would I have experienced things to share. See? It all is in God's perfect timing.

I know I have a hard head. I believe that is why it has taken so long for me to get to this place in my life. I do not know who will be reached by this book. And that is not for me to know. God told me there is a reason, and if I continue now and be obedient, this will find its place. And I may never know who it was intended for. I just say, "God, please keep me on the right path. Amen."

As I was sitting in my local church one day again wondering about my purpose and comparing myself, I heard God say again in my spirit.

"Do not stress to be more than what I want you to be, then the message I have for you will not be as I want. Continue to pray to be who you are and allow the Holy Spirit to work through you as that individual I made."

I know God loves me because he tells me over and over again not to compare, yet I do it all the time. And after all of these years, he never stopped telling me to stop, what a great example of God's unconditional love. I thank God I am better.

Paul said, "I have finished my race." When God calls us home to be with him, you know for sure your job is done as we grow into maturity with our hopes and our promises from God as described in 2 Corinthians 5:1–7.

Assurance of the Resurrection

> For we know that if our earthly house, this tent, is destroyed, we have a building from God, a house not made with hands, eternal in the heavens. For in this we groan, earnestly desiring to be clothed with our habitation which is from heaven, if indeed, having been clothed, we shall not be found naked. For we who are in this tent groan, being burdened, not because we want to be unclothed, but further clothed, that mortality may be swallowed up by life. Now He who has prepared us for this very thing is God, who also has given us the Spirit as a guarantee.
>
> So we are always confident, knowing that while we are at home in the body we are absent from the Lord. For we walk by faith, not by sight. (2 Corinthians 5:1–7, NKJV)

Chapter 3
Babe's Stage of Spiritual Growth

Old Town Lake, Lake View, Arkansas

A Babe in Christ: More about Being a Babe in Christ

In my effort to understand things for myself, I do not want to use what I call churchy words because they can be very confusing, especially when you do not have a clue of what I am talking about or what is going on. However, I believe this happens in churches a lot, especially to new believers (our babies).

When new believers are saved, sometimes as seasoned Christian we, do not realize that Christianity has its own language, and our conversations can sound like a foreign language. And because of this, we lose people who are really in need of our help/guidance. We, Christians, sometimes do not explain our terminology. I ask Father God to help us as Christians to do better in making our words clearer as we bring more and more into the family of God.

As believers, we understand each other. And at the same time leave babes, non-believers, and new believers in the dark. Over the years, I have noticed babes in Christ sometimes do not feel that they can ask questions thinking the questions would appear dumb or not wanting to appear as a person who does not know when in reality, no one knows all. I pray that my effort to simplify will indeed help someone to grow closer to God, then my task will have been completed.

Considering our babes in Christ, there is one major difference I see between a babe in Christ and a newborn baby. A newborn does not make the choice to be born where the first step to becoming a babe in Christ is a choice. It is our choice and our choice alone. As new believers, we decide that we want to follow Jesus. God does not force anyone to follow the teaching of Jesus Christ. Our creator God created us and gave us freewill of our own. On the other hand, a baby that is born in the natural realm does not choose to be born. The birth process is the way God designed it and the way it shall be. As new believers, we make our choice to follow Christ. Therefore, we should also understand that future choices we make are also ours. Becoming a believer does not mean that God take over our lives. God allows us to continue to make choices. Becoming a Christian does not take away your freewill.

I have also observed and experienced over the years that in the beginning, there is an emotional excitement that sometime comes along with being a new believer. However, we should teach that this emotional excitement does not happen to everyone, but because there may not be an emotional high when you make your decision and ask God to come into your life, it does not mean there is anything wrong. Even if you lose those emotional highs, it does not mean anything is wrong.

Each person is different. We are individuals, and if for example I am not an overly excitable person, please do not criticize me because I don't/cannot feel things the way someone else does. I can be just as overjoyed as the next person but show no excitement. This is one good reason God says not to compare ourselves as stated in scripture 2 Corinthians 10:12 (KJV):

> For we dare not make ourselves of the number, or compare ourselves with some that commend themselves: but they measuring themselves by themselves, and comparing themselves among themselves, are not wise.

Comparing is bad, and we all know new believers should have nourishment and protection as I have stated before. And in this process, learn not to compare. Sometimes when there is a loss of the spiritual excitement, there is a chance of a sudden crash in our spiritual life. And if or when this happens, there should be someone around to help us understand what happened. When no one is there to explain, it can lead to hardship or confusion. When the spiritual emotional high leaves, some new believer have thought that their salvation is lost. I learned as I grew not to base my faith on emotions because emotions come and go like the wind. Therefore, new believers need plenty of attention, encouragement, nourishment, and protection. Like a baby, we are also needing time to rest (to absorb the information provided). I know the Holy Spirit is there to help and guides us. This I will discuss a little later.

It has taken a while, but I learned that once I was saved, I was like a brand-new baby born into this world knowing nothing and having nothing with a lot to learn. Therefore, we are as the scriptures describe *babes in Christ*. According to 1 Corinthians 3:1–3 (NRSV), Paul wrote:

> And so brothers and sisters, I could not speak to you as spiritual people, but rather as people for the flesh, as infants in Christ. I fed you with milk, not solid food, for you were not ready for solid food. Even now you are still not ready for you are still of the flesh. For as long as there is jealousy and quarreling among you, are of the flesh, and behaving according to human inclinations.

As believers, we can get so excited about the good news and the joy of the Lord that new/younger believer miss the boat per say because we are not taking the time to explain better what we believe and why, especially for those with the emotional highs. We use our Christian language that new Christians and non-believers do not understand. For example, spiritual beings, our soul, and spirit—our relationship with Christ someone with whom we cannot see. (The use of these terms can be confusing)

I guess sometimes we forget what Paul said in 1 Corinthian 3:2 about "feeding with milk and not solid food for you were not ready for solid food."

We have to do better with our feeding—teaching of new believers because the best foundation is a strong foundation, and that is what we, the more mature believers, are here for.

However, to help a new believer understand, we should start early in their confession (accepting Jesus Christ as Lord and Savior). Please explain spiritual people versus the people of the flesh. Leaving this information unexplained is how we lose some new believer, but

I do understand that if we do, as the Lord has instructed, all has and will work out because the Holy Spirit is there to guide.

This reminds me that we are to plant the seed, and the Lord, will produce. Therefore, the human nature cannot understand the spiritual side because the scriptures say these two sides are always at odds with each other. Since God is Spirit, our spiritual side communicates with God from one Spirit to another. Do we initially address the two sides to new believers so not to think that once you are saved, all will be just great and not realizing that we may be saved, but we still have to continue to live in a corrupt world having freewill and negative influences all around from our enemy, Satan, and his demons?

In another version, 1 Corinthians 3:1–3 (NIV) is stated as follows:

> Brothers, I could not address you as spiritual but as worldly—mere infants in Christ I give you milk, not solid food, for you were not yet ready for it. Indeed, you are still not ready, you are worldly…

In addition to Paul, Peter wrote in 1 Peter 2:2 (NIV) which says, "Like newborn babies, crave pure spiritual milk, so that by it you may grow up in your salvation."

The scriptures state that newborn believers cannot grow unless they receive nourishment. Believers are to crave the Word of God. Newborn believers, as previously stated, should be fed as babies and continue to feed on milk which their systems can digest. Like with any baby, if they would be fed with solid food too soon, it could cause harm to the infant. Therefore, pamper new believers so as not to cause harm by trying to get them to digest solid mature material too soon. Solid food would upset an infant's system, and they may not be able to digest solid food. This is the same for babes in Christ—new believers feeding on some of the spiritual language using our spiritual lingo being too much or too confusing to actually absorb.

I notice that some beginning believers become lost, confused, and frustrated because in the beginning, no one explains that Christianity has its own language; and our conversations could sound like a foreign language as we continue to lose people who really need our help and guidance.

If we allow our believer's language can become confusing, this could cause a delay in the spiritual growth process or stop it in its tracks. For example, there could be rebellion or overload. So as babes in Christ, we should recognize that we do not mature overnight and that a lack of knowledge at this stage is natural and some hopes crushed if not treated tenderly at this point. Babes and all believers make mistakes, and many things are unclear. Therefore, the new believers need plenty of milk for strong growth before going on to eating meat. The discussion of milk means to feed on God's Word daily starting slowly to digest and absorb as to what this new thing really is, and we all should want to continue to learn as long as we live.

I would suggest that we, more learned Christians, pace ourselves to work at learning methods (how to study God Word) for ways that work for each individual, not just a one-way for all, because we all are different. I understand there are many ways that we, as people, learn; and we should be open-minded to suggestions by others.

Study the Word of God

Another thing I learned regarding our language and growth is, the first step is to study God's Word and read his guide book, the Bible. According to 2 Timothy 2:15 (KJV), it says, "Study to shew thyself approved unto God, a workman that needeth not to be ashamed, rightly dividing the word of truth."

Again, I repeat as a babe in Christ. We are newborn babies, and, to repeat myself, we cannot digest meat and potatoes. A baby starts out on milk and then baby food. I have to keep in mind that all believers, like babies, do not develop at the same levels of understanding. This principle applies to a believer's spiritual life as explained in the scriptures address at the beginning of this chapter indicate a slow start, and reading the Bible alone is not enough. According to Hebrews 5:12–14 (NIV), it states:

> In fact, thought by this time you ought to be teachers you need someone to teach you the elementary truths of God's word all over again. You need milk, not solid food! Anyone who lives on milk, being still and infant, is not acquainted with the teaching about righteousness. But solid food is for the mature, who by constant use have trained themselves to distinguish good from evil.

A babe in Christ should have protection and nourishment as a parent protects and cares for their newborn. Being taught is necessary for new believers. Being on your own will not work because Satan never rests, and he will destroy everything especially babes if given a chance. We need to teach new believers how to guard against Satan's attacks and make them aware that the attacks will come and that salvation is not an easy road to travel. A babe in Christ should be eager to learn, hungry for the Word, and should be given structured attention. There are as many stages in our personal spiritual life as there are in the natural growth process to adulthood. As we grow in Christ, there is one thing all believers should do, and that is to pray without ceasing. And *all* believers should read, study, and meditate on God's Word. And with proper structure and teaching, we will learn to live by the Spirit. According to Romans 8:5–6 (NRSV), it is as follows:

> For those who live according to the flesh set their minds on the things of the flesh, but those who live according to the Spirit set their minds on the things of the Spirit. To set the mind on the flesh is death, but to set the mind on the Spirit is life and peace.

What does this really mean? It means a believer is to study God's Word, the wonderful old testament stories, and learn of the life of Christ to understand what Jesus faced and endured while he walked this earth, and to know and understand how he handled certain situations. As we study God's Word and adhere to the teaching, we learn how to live a Christ-like life. It is a daily process. We have to study to learn and know that being Christlike is not something we do in the natural realm (religious terms).

To be Christlike requires the guidance and baptism of the Holy Spirit. With all that, I am saying I cannot emphasize enough about what works for one may not work for another. I know I should be in God's Word every day, but I am not doing as I should because some days, I can read and read and get absolutely nothing. And then on another day, I can just read one scripture, and I have something to take me through the full day. Bottom line: find what works for you, and the option of doing nothing is not an option.

"I have baptized you with water; but he will baptize you with the Holy Spirit" (Mark 1:8 NRSV). And John the Baptist in Matthew 3:13–17 (NRSV) says in the Baptism of Jesus that:

> Then Jesus came from Galilee to John at the Jordan, to be baptized by him. John would have prevented him, saying, "I need to be baptized by you, and do you come to me?"
>
> But Jesus answered him, "Let it be so now; for it is proper for us in this way to fulfill all righteousness." Then he consented. And when Jesus had been baptized, just as he came up from the water, suddenly the heavens were opened to him and he saw the Spirit of God descending like a dove and alighting on him. And a voice from heaven said, "This is my Son, the Beloved, with whom I am well pleased."

I remember being baptized in my small little town lake named the *Old Town Lake* in Lakeview, Arkansas. Back then, churches had what they called revival and designated seating for the ones who choose to follow Christ and be baptized. This would include a weeklong service of preaching generally from Sunday evening until Friday evening (each evening). Our parents would take us each night to hear the message, and it was up to us to make the decision to move to the designated seats which meant you were ready to accept Jesus Christ as your Lord and Savior publicly and be baptized. I remember making the decision to move up front, and there were others already seated. I remembered some of the others cried and had such emotional reactions. So I did not want to feel out of place, so I pretended. However, in my heart, I knew I was ready. The following Sunday, we would be baptized in the lake. We were all dressed in white robe-like outfits being escorted by a deacon out into the water, and once in place next to the preacher as he spoke a few words, then we were dunked into the water and raised quickly.

Here, again, I felt nothing, and others came up crying and praising God. For years after, I thought I missed something and needed to be rebaptized. There was so much I just did not understand, but I thank *God* for his love and learning that my salvation is not based on emotions. Please do not misunderstand me. There is nothing wrong with having emotional reactions. I just want someone who may be as I was, knowing there is nothing wrong when there is no emotional reaction. Remember, *God* made each of us different. I was not an emotional type, and my acceptance of the Lord Jesus Christ as my Lord and Savior was sufficient because the key is your acceptance of the Lord Jesus Christ as your Savior.

There is so much for a new believer to learn and never think the road is easy because it is not, and this cannot be repeated enough. Nowhere in Scripture have I found where it said the journey/race would be easy. I have such a strong feeling for new believers who have fallen away because of false hopes thinking that once I accept Jesus Christ as my Lord and Savior, heaven is the way and that life will now be all right—no problems or concerns. And when something bad/sad happens, their faith is so easily lost, and some turned their back on God.

ONCE SAVED, THEN WHAT?

I have a yearning in my heart to let doubters know the Christian life is not easy. Just think if Jesus had troubles, who are we not to have troubles? Stay strong. Keep your focus on Jesus no matter what happens—good or bad.

I think of some of the simple things in life that was used in previous generations could be revised to help little ones focus on God. And one thing I remember when I was a young girl is we would say a short prayer each night before bedtime that goes something like this: "Now I lay me down to sleep, I pray the Lord my soul to keep, if I should die before I wake I pray the Lord my soul to take."

I thank my parents for these few words I was taught and still remember. I thank them for teaching me about God and making sure I was in church and Sunday school. It hurts now that I see so many children who have never heard of Jesus and never been inside a church other than for a wedding or funeral. The crowds we used to see at Easter and Christmas have gotten smaller.

Even as a young child, I remember thinking I only want to get to heaven just get my foot through the gate. There is a lot more to it than that simple thought. As the Bible say, a child thinks like a child, but when we grow up, we leave behind the childish thoughts.

When I was a child, I spoke as a child, I understood as a child, and I thought as a child; but when I became a man, I put away childish things (1 Corinthians 13:11–13, NKJV).

As a babe in Christ, there are many things to learn, but as I study and learn, I have grown. And as long as I live, I continue to grow spiritually. As we study God's Words, it becomes a part of us. The words and message are in our hearts. As we continue to grow, we move into the second stage that I call the young adult stage. I was a babe in Christ for a long time. My growth process of understanding was very slow. (During my stages of spiritual growth, I have tried to live a Christian life. It is hard. Guess what? Life happens.) My parents taught me about heaven and hell and that both are real places. Never stop growing spiritually. Move on to the next stage *young adults in Christ*.

A Life Observation

Is it me or is it that parents have bypassed parenting and gone straight to freewill for their kids? I have seen a two-year-old in a grocery store riding on the basket and Mom asking, "What would you like?" I am a grown woman over sixty years old, and I do not know that much about nutrition even reading the boxes. How much do you think a two-year-old who cannot read would know? I am just saying.

At two years old, it would be wonderful if the parents who have given freewill to their children at the age of two or three years old would use the energy it takes to allow them to choose what to eat would give them the opportunity or guidance to choose Jesus what a blessing that would be. I know we all know this, but a two or three-year-old child needs guidance and leadership. You can see that God gave us freewill, and we can make fools of ourselves without guidance or leadership, so it is with some of our little ones. (guide the little one, do not be guided by them)

In the next section, I will include discussion of the Holy Spirit. At this point, I have learned a little more and believe I have grown to consider myself in the young adult stage.

Chapter 4
Young Adult Stage of Spiritual Growth

The falls

The second stage which I call the young adult, I think this can be the most difficult stage in a person's spiritual growth process. At this point, I knew enough to know better but not enough to know how. By this, I mean self-control. It will take time to get enough knowledge and understanding to know how to fight our major enemy (Satan) because the harder we try and study to know and get closer to Christ, the harder Satan attacks us.

In our biological growth process for our daily lives, as we mature, our responsibilities increase and the same goes for our spiritual growth. This second stage is where I identify a lot of my confusion and where my many problems erupted. This is the stage where (his/her/my) carnal side wants to keep me, but my spiritual side tells me I need to mature.

Because of these two sides, there is a constant battle inside me (all of us). I know what I need to do, but I have not studied enough to know how to get to where I really should be in my spiritual life. This is the stage where I wanted to dig deeper and try to get a better understanding of the person of the Holy Spirit. The Holy Spirit is like the wind. The wind blows, and you can feel it and see what it does; but you cannot see the wind, so it is with the Holy Spirit.

It was during this stage that I ventured out on my own not considering my action and not realizing that I do have to deal with the consequences of my actions. It is not that I forgot about my teaching. I just pushed it back in my mind. I know the Bible is true when it says to train a child in the way they should go, and they will not depart.

"Train up a child in the way he should go, and when he is old he will not depart from it" (Proverbs 22:6, MEV), and "Fathers, do not provoke your children to anger, but bring them up in the training and admonition of the Lord" (Ephesian 6:4, MEV).

I do not think I ever really left my faith. I back stepped a few times, but I always found my way back to where I belonged knowing that my God is in control, and I need to learn more and more. I remember wanting to know more about the Holy Spirit. Let me share what I found during my study.

ONCE SAVED, THEN WHAT?

In Acts 2:1–4 (NIV), it describes "the Pentecost when the apostles were all assembled and the apostles were filled with the Holy Spirit, the helper Jesus had promised would come."

> When the day of Pentecost came, they were all together in one place. Suddenly a sound like the blowing of a violent wind came from heaven and filled the whole house where they were sitting. They saw what seemed to be tongues of fire that separated and came to rest on each of them. All of them were filled with the Holy Spirit and began to speak in other tongues as the Spirit enables them.

The Holy Spirit is our helper. Over the years, I had heard that if I did not speak in tongues, I was not really saved. I do not want anyone to believe this as I did. Just because we do not or cannot speak in tongues, it does not mean that the Holy Spirit does not live inside of you as it might appear according to the scripture above alone. The gift of speaking in tongues may be there for you, and I do believe that a person can speak in tongues, and I see it as a gift because I found in the Scriptures that there are various gifts as described in 1 Corinthians 12:1–26. Therefore, speaking in tongues is a gift. The following are a lot of scriptures, but only using a part would not be clear enough.

1 Corinthians 12:1–26 (NRSV) says:

Spiritual Gifts

> Now concerning spiritual gifts, brothers and sisters, I do not want you to be uninformed. You know that when you were pagans, you were enticed and led astray to idols that could not speak. Therefore I want you to understand that no one speaking by the Spirit of God ever says

"Let Jesus be cursed!" and no one can say "Jesus is Lord" except by the Holy Spirit. (The Holy Spirit is powerful.)

Now there are varieties of gifts, but the same Spirit; and there are varieties of services, but the same Lord; and there are varieties of activities, but it is the same God who activates all of them in everyone. To each is given the manifestation of the Spirit for the common good. To one is given through the Spirit the utterance of wisdom, and to another the utterance of knowledge according to the same Spirit, to another faith by the same Spirit, to another gifts of healing by the one Spirit, to another the working of miracles, to another prophecy, to another the discernment of spirits, to another various kinds of tongues, to another the interpretation of tongues. All these are activated by one and the same Spirit, who allots to each one individually just as the Spirit chooses.

According to the scripture, the Holy Spirit provides the various kinds of tongues, and to another, it provides the ability to interpret tongues (language). My understanding is that speaking in tongues is speaking in a known language that is not your own. Therefore, as you speak, you do not know what you are saying; but during this time, your spirit is speaking to the spirit of God saying what needs to be said because the speaker really does not know what to say, therefore our helper takes over and takes care of us.

One Body with Many Members

For just as the body is one and has many members, and all the members of the body, though many, are one body, so it is with Christ.

> For in the one Spirit we were all baptized into one body—Jews or Greeks, slaves or free—and we were all made to drink of one Spirit. (Corinthians 12)

Once we are baptized in the Holy Spirit, we are a part of the same family. We are now members of the family of Jesus Christ. We are the many parts of this one family. How wonderful it is to know you are in the family with Jesus Christ. It cannot get any better than that.

> Indeed, the body does not consist of one member but of many. If the foot would say, "Because I am not a hand, I do not belong to the body," that would not make it any less a part of the body. And if the ear would say, "Because I am not an eye, I do not belong to the body," that would not make it any less a part of the body. If the whole body were an eye, where would the hearing be? If the whole body were hearing, where would the sense of smell be? But as it is, God arranged the members in the body, each one of them, as he chose. If all were a single member, where would the body be? As it is, there are many members, yet one body. The eye cannot say to the hand, "I have no need of you," nor again the head to the feet, "I have no need of you." On the contrary, the members of the body that seem to be weaker are indispensable, and those members of the body that we think less honorable we clothe with greater honor, and our less respectable members are treated with greater respect; whereas our more respectable members do not need this. But God has so arranged the body, giving the greater honor to the inferior member, that there may be no dissension within the body, but the members

> may have the same care for one another. If one member suffers, all suffer together with it; if one member is honored, all rejoice together with it.

When we are at the young adult stage of our spiritual growth, we have knowledge of what the Bible says. We know wrong from right, but our tendency to backslide appears to be great, and the desire for the world have such a big influence and pull in our lives during this stage. We are not at the point where we can face all situation will the knowledge of the Words of God. We are not at the point where we have experience enough or where we have learned enough to know how to fight our battles. And as a result, we suffer because of our lack of knowledge.

"Therefore, My people go into exile for their lack of knowledge; and their honorable men are famished, and their multitude is parched with thirst" (Isaiah 5:13).

I correlate this to when I turned twenty-one years of age, and like many youths, I believed I knew everything. I now know how much I needed to learn to deal with my real enemy, the devil. I remember being told that I was too young to know what it was. I didn't know that at the time, it made no sense, but time brings about change and knowledge.

Now I know the devil knows how to mess with us all the time. He stopped me so many times from my assignment. I did not know then what was happening. I have learned that the devil attacks often and always contrary to what is right. When I was getting started on this project the latest time, it seemed everywhere I go, people were talking about the same information I wanted to write about. I would begin to question myself, what do I have to say? For example, one Sunday, there was an announcement in church that a young lady had written a book and is working to get it published. And immediately, there I was thinking, *What am I trying to do? Should I just give up this idea?*

There is nothing new I can say, but this time, I said "No, Devil. Not this time. I am going to move forward because my Father told me he had plans for my assignment, and it got a little clearer because God knows I have such a hard head."

The thing here is that I did not know what the other person's book was about or anything, but Satan came up with negative thoughts. At times of frustration and confusion, the sinful nature in us is working overtime. I believe we fall into traps, bad situations, and make bad decisions. We allow it because our freewill is leaning in the direction of that sinful nature. At this point, we do not know enough to really separate the sinful nature from the spiritual, and it can be difficult, believe me. The pull of the world and Satan is very strong. By accepting the practices of this world, we allow ourselves to be influenced by this sinful world. The Lord never takes away our freewill, so the directions we take and the decisions we make are all ours own, and I know now that I cannot blame anyone but myself for the many decisions I have made—good and bad.

Finally, I know I can only blame my bad choices on myself for not doing as I should. I did not take the time necessary to study God's Word. I would get lonely and start to search for something I already had. I was feeling tired of everything because I would feel like a failure to God. None of these are good excuses. There are no good excuses. I start telling myself, *How am I to know who is telling the truth? That Church is too small. This church is too large and too far away.* All of these are useless and unnecessary excuses. However, I learned through prayers and asking God for guidance and following through. I always eventually found myself where I was supposed to be. I always found that local church, and, by this, I know it was the Holy Spirit at work in my life. We cannot make it without *him* (the Holy Spirit).

A bright thought I once believed that when I became a new person in Christ, born again with the Holy Spirit inside, God would eliminate everything in my life that was not perfect. I thought there would be visible changes in me, physically, emotionally, and mentally. I do not think that way anymore. I know that I am and always will be who *God* made me to be, but I know that I am not alone. (Oh, God, I hope this helps someone if only one that in itself will be a success).

From my study, it finally sinks in that our bodies are the houses where the Holy Spirit resides, but the Holy Spirit is not here to overpower my freewill that God originally gave me as a human being. I learned that I should relay on the Spirit more according to Galatians 5:16–18 (NIV). Paul's letter to the Galatians states that:

> So I say, live by the Spirit, and you will not gratify the desires of the sinful nature. For the sinful nature desires what is contrary to the Spirit, and the Spirit what is contrary to the sinful nature. They are in conflict with each other, so that you do not do what you want. But if you are led by the Spirit, you are not under law.

It took time, but I learned. I know and understand that I am saved, and I know that the Holy Spirit lives within. I used to wonder why my life has so many struggles within. I now know about the constant struggle within between my spirit and my human nature (desires) as described by Paul's writing in Galatians 5:16–17 (NRSV):

> Live by the Spirit, I say and do not gratify the desires of the flesh. For what the flesh desire is opposed to the spirit, and what the spirit desires is opposed to the flesh; for these are opposed to each other, to prevent you from doing what you want.

The above scripture explains the why to this battle we have inside. I found in my studies and explanation that discussed living by the Holy Spirit powers that I think is good and something to think about as a believer, and it also helped in my understanding. The notes in the Life Application Bible for Galatians 5:16–18 are:

> The character traits that are found in the nature of Christ then we should know the Holy Spirit is leading us. However, "At the same time,

> be careful not to confuse your feeling with the Spirit's leading. Being led by the Holy Spirit involves the desires to hear, the readiness to obey God's word, and the sensitivity to discern between your feeling and his prompting's. Live each day controlled and guided by the Holy Spirit. Then the words of Christ will be in your mind, the love of Christ will be behind your actions, and the power of Christ will help you control your selfish desires.

I found this information and wording to be very clear and understanding. It seems to lay out the truth. It opened my mind to rely on the Lord and adhere to the guidance of the Holy Spirit, and I would not go wrong.

The Holy Spirit will never lead us in the wrong direction. It is our responsibility to allow the Holy Spirit to lead us. For example, think of the Holy Spirit in this scenario. You invite a person into your home to make repairs. You open the door to let him in, but you leave him standing at the door. This person knows why he is there, but he needs you to allow him to do his job, but he needs openness from you.

However, you continue on with your everyday activities and forget that you opened the door to let him in. You would not expect this person to just take over your home because if he did, you would resist and object emphatically. So if you let them in, please let them do their job (allow the Holy Spirit to do his within you). We invite the Holy Spirit into our lives when we accepted Jesus Christ as our Savior. In 2 Corinthians 1:21–22 (NRSV), it says, "But it is God who established us with you in Christ and has anointed us, by putting his seal on us and giving us his Spirit in our hearts as a first installment."

When we are saved, and the Holy Spirit comes into our lives. We should not forget we have invited company. Therefore, when the Holy Spirit comes into our lives, we should give him free reign over the property which is us and not hinder the progress. The Holy Spirit comes into our lives knowing what we need and what repairs are necessary. The Holy Spirit is in tune to God's will for our lives. If we keep out of the way, the Holy Spirit can fulfill his mission. In Titus 3:5–8 (NRSV), we find these words:

> He saved us, not because of any works of righteousness that we had done, but according to his mercy, through the water of rebirth and renewal by the Holy Spirit. This Spirit he poured out on us richly through Jesus Christ our Savior, so that, having been justified by his grace, we might become heirs according to the hope of eternal life. The saying is sure.

We must remember also that we can hinder the Holy Spirit. It was during this stage that I did *not* know enough not to hinder the Holy Spirit, and Satan knows this and will come at us from all directions. Another thing I learned is that we should not grieve the Holy Spirit as stated in Ephesians 4:30 (NRSV): "Do not grieve the Holy Spirit of God, by whom you were sealed for the day of redemption," and in 1 Thessalonians 5:17–19 (NRSV), it states, "Pray without ceasing, give thanks in all circumstance; for this is the will of God in Christ Jesus for you. Do not quench the Spirit."

In this stage, I caused much confusion and problems for myself. The scripture in Hebrews 5:12–14 (NIV) really addressed where I found myself during this stage.

> In fact, though by this time you ought to be teachers you need someone to teach you the elementary truth of God's word all over again. You need milk, not solid food! Anyone who lives on milk, being still and infant, is not acquainted with the teaching about righteousness. But solid food is for the mature, who by constant use have trained themselves to distinguish good from evil. (Hebrews 5:12–14, NIV)

This applies because I fell between needing milk and digesting solid food. I had not learned enough to know what to do with solid food or trained by practice to distinguish good from evil although I though at the time, I had. I was always thinking I knew more than I really did, but with time and living long enough, I learned.

However, to grow from an infant through maturity, we must learn discernment. We must train ourselves, our minds, and our bodies to distinguish right from wrong. We should train ourselves about the correct use of scripture from mistaken use and recognize temptation before it traps us.

Another description I found that describes the growth process I liked was from the *notes* in the NIV Life Application Bible for Hebrews 5:14. It says, "Our capacity to feast on deeper knowledge of God (solid food) is determine by our spiritual growth. Too often we want God's banquet before we are spiritually capable of digesting it."

As we grow in the Lord and put into practice what we have learned, our capacity to understand will grow even greater. I think this statement really describes this stage of spiritual growth. We think we are there, but in reality, we have ways to go.

I have, and we should invite the Holy Spirit in and give him free reign. The Holy Spirit knows what work is necessary but cannot do his work if we are always in the way. There is another point I think should be discussed here, and that is believers should know that the Holy Spirit is not the only Spirit. The Bibles warn of other spirits, and the bible also tells us how to test the spirits. We should know how to test the spirits. In my studies, I came across the scripture that discusses this. And it appears to me that knowing to test could help a believer know that all guidance and information we hear may not be from God. The testing of the spirits and knowing that we should distinguish truth from false teachings is described in 1 John 4:1–6 (NIV):

> Dear friends, do not believe every spirit, but test the spirit to see whether they are from God, because many false prophets have gone out into the world. This is how you can recognize

> the Spirit of God; Every spirit that acknowledges that Jesus Christ has come in the flesh is from God, but every spirit that does not acknowledge Jesus is not from God. This is the spirit of the antichrist, which you have heard is coming and even now is already in the world.

I think that when I was in this stage, I got complacent with myself. I began to think I was just fine. I became comfortable with just hearing a sermon mostly each week. I had gotten comfortable with only having the desire to hear and be entertained with regular church services. I had convinced myself that I was doing good and all was just fine. Little did I know.

As I have previously said, I find this to be a most difficult stage because Satan is more aware of our condition than we are, and he uses all kinds of methods to attack us. For example, Satan can use the Word of God on us; and we will even condemn ourselves if we are not prayerful and discerning toward good and evil and without knowing that there is false teaching and not discerning what we hear and read. I believe that prayer is a major key in a believer's life. As the scriptures say in Romans 8:26–27 (NASB):

> And in the same way the Spirit also helps our weakness; for we do not know how to pray as we should, but the Spirit himself intercedes for us with groanings too deep for words, and he who searches the hearts knows what the mind of the spirit is, because he intercedes for the saints according to the will of God.

Encounter with the Holy Spirit

During my early years, I was not taught much about speaking/praying in tongues, but I had read and heard about it. When I was in my late twenties to early thirties, working in the Chicago, Illinois, area, I had a habit of getting to work early and going to the bathroom being alone with my journal for quite time to pray and start my day as I wrote about my concerns and issues. As always, I was a member and attending a local church regularly and active as the bookkeeper and usher.

Well, one particular morning, I was in the bathroom alone—praying and writing—and the Holy Spirit took control of my tongue, and I know I was speaking in a language I did not understand, and I could not control my tongue. It was as if my mouth was on its own, and when it finished, I was so filled with joy I could hardly contain myself. I was standing in the bathroom stall wishing for more of this experience. I believe I was speaking in tongues. It was definitely an unknown language for me. I know I was in a state where I really did not know what to pray, so the Spirit was praying to *God* for me because I knew not what to say. It was a feeling I cannot explain. It was a joy I cannot express. We can tell others of our encounters, but there is nothing like having the experience for yourself. Being alone, I am aware that there was no need for interpretation; only my spirit and God needed to know what was needed.

In writing this, I realized that some people are probably spiritual enough and know this, and what I am saying may sound simple because some people probably have encounters often; but for me, this was very special. It does not happen often, but when it does, I really cannot express the joy and peace it brings to my heart. I know I am not alone on this issue, and there are some who just needed to hear about my particular encounter. And to you, keep praying, reading, and trusting. Our Lord is never far away. I said before I am not trying to reach the already reached. I am trying to help others who may have backed away, given up thinking that it is too hard, or simply saying to themselves, what is the point in all of this religious stuff? To you, I say there is truly a point.

You may have heard others say to "press on. God is with you. Read the Bible every day, pray, and ask God for understanding. Have faith. It's going to be alright. And once you have Jesus in your life, everything will be okay because God will give you peace."

From my experience, I believe having faith, praying, reading, and studying does not do it for everyone, and it will not bring peace to everyone who tries it. I do believe God does not see any one person better than the other because he made us all. But God does see each one as the person he has made. Each individual has to work toward what works for them.

There is nothing in this world that will have the exact same affect or impact on everyone because not one of us are exactly alike, not even twins. However, what works for me may not work for someone else, but we will not know unless we try. My point in all of this is for you not to feel that you failed because something did not work for you. What you have to do is try something else or a different way because when you find it, you will know. Amen.

I do not want to load up on a lot of things that will do this or that because this or that, I do not know. I can only say keep trying—never give up, never give up.

In all that I may have said, there is one thing I know for sure. God loves us all, and Jesus paid the ultimate price to give us an opportunity to have a relationship with our Father God in heaven, and I thank Jesus with all my heart.

The Relationship

We hear believers all the time talking about having a relationship with Jesus Christ our Lord and Savior. In order to get to know Jesus Christ, we have to develop what believers call a relationship. A relationship with God is like any relationship. It is a growing process. It has to develop, and as everything, all relationships are not the same. Our enemy, Satan, does not want you to establish this relationship; and he works hard to stop you and distract you and confuse you. Our spiritual growth is the developing of our relationship with Christ.

When I was a child, I would hear people say, "God spoke to me." I was under the impression that they heard an audible voice from heaven, and I wanted to hear that voice. Life teaches that is not the normal because I believe that if God wanted to verbally speak, he would do just that. However, my experience over the years has been a very low whisper in my spirit (mind). Some say it was my conscious, so I believe God uses our conscious (spirit) as one way to speak to us. If only we would listen.

There have been times when I was sitting and reading my daily devotional and the Bible or writing a prayer to God in my journal, and it would be as if I started having this conversation in my mind. I know it is God because it is always soft, kind, and loving even when it is a reprimand. I have a short attention span, so I never have long conversations. I hear the message, and he is gone. I also know and believes with all my heart that God, through small soft voice, would never tell me to do anything wrong because I know right from wrong. Praise God for speaking to me as I write.

Because of my relationship, I received directions from Jesus Christ through our helper. He sent us in the person of the Holy Spirit. For example, while I was writing at one point, I was trying to figure out the organization of my separate notes. And God said, "Now is not the time to think about organization. Keep writing, and when it is time, it all will be put in place." This made so much sense. I knew it was Jesus. Therefore, I put organization behind and concentrated more on getting the words on paper.

When I first started, my focus was on a book. As I said before, I was searching for answers for myself, and it really was not going to be a book. It was a message as I had thought God had told me. Mostly everything has been written in long hand and were typed up later. Somehow, this works for me. When a thought comes, I have to write it down. And once I get these thoughts out on papers, as God said, someone will help me put it in order. Then it will make good sense to anyone reading. To know and understand the relationship with Jesus, my Lord and Savior, God can use any circumstance to get us back on track.

Because of my relationship, as I think back, I can see where Jesus has worked in my life many times. For another example, I have never been a person who was long-winded outside of talking to my close friends and family. I had the mind-set to state the facts and go because I did not like the sound of my own voice. The idea of writing a book was ridiculous. How could I ever find enough words? We never know what situation or circumstance God will use. Well, when I was working in Washington, DC, I joined the organization called *Toastmasters* to learn how to speak better. It really is a good organization for that purpose. I joined and ended up competing right off at our local level, and, behold, I won, adlibbing which is what the contest was about. For a person who did not like to hear my own voice went on to win the division level. I also became the local chapter president. I grew with this organization faster and better than I had ever believed or done before. I got my confidence in myself back. Prior to this, I was ready to give up. I felt my prayers were not being answered. I had made the wrong decisions to move to the Washington, DC, area, and it was all beginning to fall in on me.

However, after one of my presentations, a lady in the audience walked up to me and asked, "Are you a minister?" And of course, I had to tell her *no* and far from it, but she said my presentation was like a sermon to her. That was not my intention to sound that way, but it shows how what you say can be received so differently. I included this story to say to those of us who think you have no talent or nothing to do to serve God to not ever give up. It may take some time, but one day, you will hear God speak. And you will hear and learn about the gift God has given you, and it is up to us to use it. I truly was a mess because for years, I kept asking God, *what am I supposed to be doing?* I thought it had to be something really special, and I realized it was to simply live the life God had given me. And God had told me over and over again to *stop* comparing myself to others. By not listening to *God*, it caused me to be confused and not take time to hear what he was saying to me. In establishing your relationship with God, remember that Satan will work to stop you at every turn with distractions. And for me, through joining an organization, I got my confidence and hope back which Satan tried to take away.

Through my experiences and developing my relationship with Christ, I have learned about a few of Satan's distractions. Satan will definitely attack during prayer. I have wanted to pray for people, and before I get started, I can't remember the names, or I write the names down, and before I get going, my mind started to wonder on all sorts of things. I know I have a short attention span, and I cannot sit anywhere for hours and have complete concentration on what's going on. I lose interest fast, but I have learned how to get myself to refocus.

Do not let your mind wander too long. This is one example of how the devil can cause us to want to give up. To recognize this is happening is not easy, and when you do get to the point where you can recognize, it is a good step. Because of these distractions, I caused myself to think badly of myself, and I wondered many times about what was wrong with me. Why could I not stay focused? It was not me per say—it was that spiritual team battling all the time. The best way to get to know about *God* is to read about him. Do not be one with a lack of knowledge.

Reading

Still, talking about relationship with God, we have to get to know a person to better our relationship. And with *God*, we need to read what God has for us to read to get to know him. Satan attacks me every time I try to get into a reading routine. The devil has attacked (confused) me and kept me with the wrong thinking. For example, has anyone ever read the Bible on a reading plan and actually completed it, and after all that reading, you cannot remember one single thing you've read? Well, I know someone—me. How about doing less daily reading? For example, the Bible in two years with the same results and remember nothing. Well, you are right. It is me.

When it comes to reading the Bible, I could not really understand everything. I was reading the Bible years ago, and I remember one Sunday afternoon at home with just my mom and myself, and I got the Bible and wanted to read out loud to my mom, and she would always say "go ahead that would be just fine." On this particular Sunday, I cannot remember what I was reading, but at one point, I said to my mother that I just didn't understand what I had just read. And my mother said this to me years ago, "There are certain times when God will reveal a clear understanding of certain things to us. God only allows us to understand what we can handle at certain times in our lives." I had a wise mom.

God reveals to us what we need when we need it. Over the years, as I have read the same scriptures, there has been a different little nugget I've understood over the years. So if I read the entire Bible and remembered or understood nothing, I have learned to keep reading and one day what God has for me to understand will occur. I learned that Satan or one of his fallen angels was always around to make an effort to corrupt my thinking, and many times, it caused me to withdraw. I thank God for my parents who started me out right as the Bible says, "Train up a child in the way he should go; and when he is old, he will not depart from it" (Proverbs 22:6, KJV).

It does not say the child would not venture off and get lost, but with the imbedded knowledge as a child, they can find their way back to Jesus as I have experienced during my lifetime.

There are so many more examples of ways on how Satan attacks us and tries to keep us confused. The point is to learn to recognize the attacks and take defensive actions.

Peace

When there is confusion, this is not of *God* because in 1 Corinthians 14:33, (NASB) it says, "For God is not the author of confusion, but of peace, as in all churches of the saints," and Philippians 4:7 (NIV) says, "And the peace of God, which transcends all understanding, will guard your hearts and your minds in Christ Jesus."

My peace is and has been interrupted many times, and this is one thing you will hear me repeat over and over about God reminding me not to compare myself to others. I am a very hard-headed person because I keep doing it. Praise God for he does not give up on me.

I was reading my daily devotional one morning, and it was *God* telling me it was time to get back to my assignment, and again, he told me to tell my story concerning reading his Word, which I have.

But I do remember especially the part where each person learns and remembers differently that what works for one does not always work for the other. We should all search and listen to others but find what works for you as you pray and ask *God* for guidance and wisdom.

As we grow and continue to learn, we move into what I call the third stage—the stage of being mature in Christ.

Chapter 5

An Effort Toward Maturity in Spiritual Growth

The Washington Monument

As I begin to look at what I call the *mature stage*, I see this as the point where a Christian has developed or is developing the best understanding of *God* and can recognize their real relationship with the Father through the Son, Jesus Christ, by the Holy Spirit resulting in a single relationship that will continue to grow until the day we die.

Like all relationships, there has to be good communication. We continue to get closer and closer to *God* through prayer and supplication, meditation, and being quiet. It is during my quiet time when the message from *God* is clear. However, I can be busy, and if there is something that I must hear, believe me, it comes through. Remember all things are possible for *God*. Another thing I found out is that our communication can be stalled because the scriptures tell us *not* to grieve the Holy Spirit, and our communication is, by and through the Holy Spirit, whom Jesus sent to help us as discussed in Ephesians 4:30–31 (NIV):

> Don't cause the Holy Spirit sorrow by the way you live. Remember, he is the one who marks you to be present on that day when salvation from sin will be complete.
>
> Stop being mean, bad-tempered, and angry. Quarreling, harsh words, and dislike of others should have no place in your lives. Instead, be kind to each other, tenderhearted, forgiving one another, just as God has forgiven you because you belong to Christ.

Also, in 1 Thessalonian 5:16–24, (NIV) the scripture says:

> Rejoice always, pray continually, give thanks in all circumstances; for this is God's will for you in Christ Jesus. Do not quench the Spirit. Do not treat prophecies with contempt but test them all; hold on to what is good, reject every kind of evil.

> May God himself, the God of peace, sanctify you through and through. May your whole spirit, soul and body be kept blameless at the coming of our Lord Jesus Christ. The one who calls you is faithful, and he will do it.

A mature believer, in my opinion, is one who has more understanding regarding God's Word and a stronger ability of communicating. In all reality, we are never grown up in Christ because our understanding can never reach the complete understanding of all of God's Word. I believe there is always something new to learn in Christ, and we can never comprehend all that God has because we have such limitations as human beings.

This stage is the one I am working to reach. I want to get to the point where I have a stronger relationship and discipline to hear from *God* often and the ability to help others with what I receive. I know my attention span is not very long. And the one thing I have done for many, many years, and that is, as I mentioned before, I write prayers all the time to God in journals. When I try to just talk to God, my mind strays quickly; but if I write, it helps me concentrate. And my mind does not stray as much. I considered my written prayer as letters to God, and when you write a letter to anyone which we do not do anymore, we have the opportunity to think about what we want to say. It helps me keep focused on who I am talking to and helps me focus on what I want and need to say.

In this day and age, we have so many electronic ways to communicate and keep in touch with each other. I have a *Facebook* account, and I see where many people use it to display words of encouragement, and others use words of destruction, and you can instantly message people. This destruction grows rapidly and is impossible to contain. I would say during this time, remember that no matter what the enemies' tactics are, we, as Christians, know who is truly in control—our Father who art in heaven. If you are old enough to remember receiving a hand-written letter from someone years ago, it was a joy, pleasing, and comforting. We used to keep personal letters because we could reread them later, and it would help us remember when we can reread our electronic messages, but I want to relay the message that if you find it difficult to pray, try writing a personal letter to God.

As I write my letters to God, I believe he hears my heart. And during this time, it is when I feel the closeness. Father God in heaven, thanks for all you do, and let these words be a blessing to someone one day. I am asking in the name of your only Son, Jesus the Christ. Amen.

Maturity is a struggle and a hard place to get to. I know this because if Paul, who was chosen by God, had a hard time, then who am I to complain? The following is a list I compiled of things I know how to do but do not do. However, I have learned my battle is not with flesh and blood but, as the writer of Ephesians described in Ephesians 6:12 (TLB), it is:

> For we are not fighting against people made of flesh and blood, but against persons without bodies the evil rulers of the unseen world, those mighty satanic beings and great evil prince of darkness who rule this world; and against huge numbers of wicked spirits in the spirit world.

I know I should not be guilt-ridden because I have not done things I should but realized that every day of my life will be a struggle. I have to share the things I know to do, and yet I do not. This is to say, "You are not alone in this. We all have this battle to fight."

Things I Do Not Do as I Should

1. I do not pray as I should.
2. I do not read the Bible as I should, and each year, I promise to do better, and it lasts only for a little while.
3. I do not read my daily devotionals every day.
4. I do not keep Jesus first on my mind every day.
5. I do not always consult with God on all decisions I have to make.

I could go on and on with longer lists because I am not where I want to be, but this is where I want to get to, and that is maturity in Christ; therefore, I can say this is my hope and goal as I express my thoughts to you. God knows who he made in the person of me and you. He has given us instructions and guidance—his Word (the Bible)—to help us, and that's why with all my faults and because of God's love and grace, I know I am a child of God; and I will see Jesus because my God forgives when I ask for forgiveness, and my God love me completely and unconditionally when I accepted his Son, Jesus the Christ, as my Lord and Savior. However, I will be punished for my disobedience, and, at the same time, because of my lack, I will have missed out on some blessings. Remember, God knows our hearts. The real person of who we all are is in the heart, and that is the part of us that no other humans can see or know what is in our hearts other than our Lord and Savior. Praise God.

As long as we live and reach for maturity in Christ, our enemy will be working to defeat us. If Paul, who was used by God, can write of conflicts within, then how could we ever think we can live without conflicts? I know we hear people say "trust in the Lord and everything will be all right." Yes, it will but not without a battle. Satan wants to keep us confused, and living a Christian-believing life is not easy. Paul tells us all about it in Romans 7 that describes himself being pulled between two different places. I have had many days as described by Paul in Romans 7:14–25 as follows from the Message Bible version (MSG).

> I know that all God's commands are spiritual, but I'm not. Isn't this also your experience? Yes. I'm full of myself—after all, I've spent a long time in sin's prison. What I don't understand about myself is that I decide one way, but then I act another, doing things I absolutely despise. So if I can't be trusted to figure out what is best for myself and then do it, it becomes obvious that God's command is necessary.

> But I need something more! For if I know the law but still can't keep it, and if the power of sin within me keeps sabotaging my best intentions, I obviously need help! I realize that I don't have what it takes. I can will it, but I can't do it. I decide to do good, but I don't really do it; I decide not to do bad, but then I do it anyway. My decisions, such as they are, don't result in actions. Something has gone wrong deep within me and gets the better of me every time.

I know that God does not look for perfect people to use nor people who gives the appearance of knowing it all because when God calls, he equips you to do what he called you to do. Just think that Paul was called and equipped, but he still had concerns and problems as he continued to write in the following verses of Romans 7:21–23 (MSG) as written in scripture verses below:

> …happens so regularly that it's predictable. The moment I decide to do good, sin is there to trip me up. I truly delight in God's commands, but it's pretty obvious that not all of me joins in that delight. Parts of me covertly rebel, and just when I least expect it, they take charge.
>
> I've tried everything and nothing helps. I'm at the end of my rope. Is there no one who can do anything for me? Isn't that the real question?
>
> The answer, thank God, is that Jesus Christ can and does. He acted to set things right in this life of contradictions where I want to serve God with all my heart and mind but am pulled by the influence of sin to do something totally different.

Therefore, I can truly say, "Know and believe that this battle I have is not with flesh and blood but with this worlds prince of darkness, and the best thing is that I know my battle has already been won, and so has yours." During these battles, excuses will not work because God my Father in heaven sees everything I do and hears every word I say. But because of his love and grace, he forgives me, yet punishes me for my own good like any good parent would do to their child. With all the things I do not do, there are things I have gotten better at over the years as I have learned to do better, and it's all due to the grace and love of my Father in heaven. All is never lost.

Let me remind the readers again these words are for someone who may be having concerns with Christian language and are young at heart and are trying to understand. I am reaching for the babies to help understand that this battle is within and growth is a process. We human are either carnal or spiritual by nature. The term *carnal* I will define as a human being existing without the Spirit of God (Holy Spirit) living inside of them but living by their own thoughts and belief and that everything I do or accomplish, I have done solely under my own powers and totally depends on oneself.

We are not and do not have to depend on oneself because the Father sent us a helper and comforter. According to the scripture, Jesus sent the Holy Spirit back to dwell inside of us as described on the day of Pentecost in Acts 2:1–4, and in John 14:26 (TLB), Jesus said, "But when the Father sends the Comforter instead of me—and the Comforter I mean the Holy Spirit—he will teach you much, as well as remind you of everything I myself have told you."

This can be a very complex subject, and yet it's not. I know if we have a relationship with Jesus by reading and studying God's Word, he will show us understanding at our own pace through our helper and comforter, the Holy Spirit. Amen.

However, we can and do interject confusion because *God* gave each of us a freewill to think and do as we please. Our decisions and words are a choice. It is our choice to follow Jesus or not. I am repeating things I have said over and over again, but sometimes, we need to hear things over and over to get a clear understanding. I think of myself and how I need to hear things repeated to simply understand, and with the enemy, we, as Christians, have to stay strong and repeat as well as being in constant prayer.

I have discussed the Holy Spirit before, but I asked God, "How do I explain the person of the Holy Spirit any way other than how it has been explained for years?" And the Bible is so clear. How can I make anything simple and clear when it is already simple and clear? I heard these words, "You cannot, but remember this information is for someone who may not have heard what I am giving you to write." Therefore, I shall continue as I feel being led by the Lord.

The Holy Spirit that lives inside of us is how the Father communicates with us. Our spirit connects to the Father's Spirit for us, and when we are led by our inner spirit, we are allowing our Father to use us and guide us, and when it is truly our Father leading, you will know because our Father would never lead you/us to do or say anything that would be harmful, especially anything that would not give glory and honor to the Father. There is so much that can be said about the Holy Spirit, but simply, he is one of the triune God, our one and only living God. We have God the Father, God the Son, and God the Holy Spirit.

Life's Journey

The Dan Ryan Expressway in Chicago

As I was thinking about this journey of life, it really is a journey. It's a journey to learn who Jesus really is and a journey to get to know God and await the time when we will hear Jesus Christ say "Well done, my good and faithful servant" as written by Paul the Apostle in 2 Timothy 4:6–8 NIV:

> For I am already being poured out like a drink offering, and the time for my departure is near. I have fought the good fight, I have finished the race, I have kept the faith. Now there is in store for me the crown of righteousness, which the Lord, the righteous Judge, will award to me on that day—and not only to me, but also to all who have longed for his appearing.

Father God, I believe you have told me to write this. And I now know that you are telling me it is time to finish it. God, I cannot finish it without you. I need you to guide me and keep me focused on what you want me to say. I want with all my heart to finish this task, but I just cannot see me having enough words for a book, but I know this is where my faith in God's guidance comes in.

To reach for maturity, we have to venture through life's trial and errors but never cut God short. He can and will use whomever he chooses to do his will. You just could be one of the ones.

Including myself, I know better. But I and others have treated the love of God as our genie in the bottle or Santa Clause, thinking that when in need, God should come now. I have found it hard to help some people understand that God is neither Santa Clause nor a genie in a bottle or a magician. I say this because I have known a few people who act like that is what God is or should be.

For example, I have heard people saying nothing about Father God when things are going well. The people I refer to say they truly believe that God exists and is all-powerful, but they do not think there is anything they must do but believe. However, having faith and believing is the key, but it is not a selfish-life journey. We are to become like Jesus. When things go bad and, in most cases, it is because of our own bad decision, we cry out to our Father and ask for help. Some look for a miracle to happen immediately and help them out. And when the answer they wanted does not come when they want it, the responses have been awful.

I know a few people who have cursed (God) and said there is no God because God did not do what they wanted when they wanted. Then there are those of us who want to help, and we tell them to pray and ask God for help and guidance. We are giving spiritual advice to non-spiritual persons. I am asking God right now to help who may be reading this that the right words for clarity be used. I know the religious answers, but I want something that will help the unlearned to understand and how they are to look to God. I am looking for words that will penetrate that negative way of thinking. I want this to make sense to the ones who are blind to who our Lord and Savior really is and what he should mean to us.

During my efforts in writing, I am learning that for sure, no one needs to be a perfect person to be used by God. And as I said many times before as God had told me many times before, what I see someone else do is not necessarily what he has for me to do and to stop beating myself over the head saying, "Why can't I do like them, pray like them, speak like them, read, and be as dedicated as someone else?" And God always say, "I made you to be you and you alone if I wanted you to pray like them or speak like them. I would have made you them." I would think I would get it right by now but not me. The enemy knows my weakness and stays on top of them.

Please understand that we have to continue to remind ourselves (especially me) over and over again because the devil keeps bringing it to mind that I need to do more, pray more, read more, and study more. But Father, the more I try, the less I do. And for me, the less I understand, the more I read and read and remember nothing. I want to let others know that there is nothing wrong when we cannot be like others. I was encouraged by my local Pastor James Butler, also not to compare, he told me to continue to "listen to what God has for you."

You cannot remember everything you read, but we must stay in communication through conversations and prayer with God to learn what it is that he has for us to do. I used to think that because I pray short prayers and read short passages, there was something missing because others could pray long prayers and quote the scriptures. But God told me several times and, I repeat again, because someone's head may be as hard as mine. God said to stop comparing and that he knows what is within our hearts that I am a child of God, and he is watching over me. I make mistakes, and I screw up a lot, but I learned not to feel guilty because I have not done as others. But we are to do as the Bible said to study and show ourselves approved, study, and meditate on God's Words as written in Joshua 1:8 (NRSV).

> This book of the law shall not depart out of your mouth; you shall meditate on it day and night, so that you may be careful to act in accordance with all that is written in it. For then you shall make your way prosperous, and then you shall be successful.

If you have been in my position of confusion, I do not want anyone to get the idea that they do not need to do anything because that is not the message I am trying to relay. I want others not to be as I was, not to think hard of yourself, and to understand this type of reaction because this type of reaction is covered in the scriptures as written by Paul who said the things "I know to do I do not" as previously discussed in Romans chapter 7:17–25 in this book in chapter 4. We cannot do anything without the Holy Spirit that Jesus sent back when he returned to sit on the right hand of God the Father. We really cannot do anything on our own. We need to be filled with the Spirit. We need, above all, to have a relationship with Christ as previously discussed.

My Personal Steps

My first step was to have faith, believe, and study to learn who God is and how to get to know God for myself. As I said before, this relationship is a process that will last an entire lifetime, and there is nothing you can accomplish on your own without including other believers in your life. We are to hear God's Word, and he gave us a book to read from which we learn that despite some of the hardships we go through, we can make it through. The Scriptures never said it would be easy, but we have to believe and trust in the Lord. No man is an island and can survive only on his own. It takes faith, love, understanding, trust, and not just believing but knowing that God is alive, and he knows and sees all.

My second step was to talk with God. We need to make time for God. Talking to God is not always through prayer. It can be as having a conversation telling God your concerns, hopes, and desires. Just imagine if you are a parent and how wonderful it is when your child comes to you and just talk about their ideas, plans, hopes, and dreams. With Father God, it is the same take time to talk to him out loud or simply in our minds. He hears our desires and knows our hearts. Jesus is interceding for us who belong to him every day.

Talk to God every day even only for a few minutes. He does not need to hear your life story. He knows it already. He just wants you to come to him as your Father and say, "I want to talk to you. Father God, can we have a few minutes?"

Sometimes, you can just be quiet, and your Father God in heaven hears your heart and spirit. The peace that you can get will surpass all that you have ever experienced.

I am here to tell you *God is real*, and he just wants your attention—respectful attention. God does not want your rude, disrespectful attitude. He wants your love and respect as you come into his presence, and like any Father, he wants his child to come to him with respect, love, and having a good time in his presence. Remember, just because you talk to God once, it does not mean he is your lucky charm because he is not. He is still your Father who wants the best for you, but if you keep making decisions without asking him first, you will continue to have the same problems as before. As the saying goes, "the same actions cause the same results. If you want change, change actions."

Consult our Father in heaven before any decision no matter how small you may think it is. God loves us so much and want us to use our own judgment to come to him because he gives us freewill to make up our own minds; but when you go to him, he is here to help you but only if he knows you intimately. Do not try to be slick and put God to a test. The one who gets tested will be you, and you will be the one who loses.

As I continue, it may sound confusing because God is love, and he knows all; but then I say you need to talk to him. The question may be, why talk when he already knows everything? An example would be as follows: think about a Father who already knows his son or daughter had banged up the car, but he is waiting to see if they will come to him with the truth. And when they do, how wonderful he feels that they think enough of him and feel that they can come directly to him and let him know what happened. This is the same with our heavenly Father. Go to the Father will all your desires, concerns, and hopes.

Another question maybe, why do I have to ask when he already knows what I need? Let's look at as if a mother/father knows that their child needs a hundred dollars but are waiting for the child to come and ask. I am not talking about a time when their child is always asking. I mean one who had been independent, and there is truly a need; not just a want, and the child has the faith to go to the parents honestly and ask, at the same time, explaining the need. The parents, without a doubt, would be willing to help to keep their child strong and not weak by giving into their every whim. I guess what I am trying to say is look at our Father in heaven, our God, as the loving parent we all have. He is waiting for us to realize that is who he is.

Although I continued to pray as I continued with this book, I have continually felt the pull of negativity. This is why I have to ask Father God to keep giving me the words to write and the ability to complete this task and reach the people God said it would. There are millions of people and millions of books, but I believe I have been given this project; and I will continue to pray to God that I get it completed and accomplish what it is he wants me to accomplish and not be hardheaded and give up because every day, there are distractions to make me want to stop. However, I know I am not to give up. I know I will have to continue to pray to be able to make it through Satan's attacks, problems, and changes. Although in the past, I have gotten myself into some deep difficult situations that could have been avoided. If only I had paid attention to God through prayer. In our lifetimes, things happen; and I have, on occasions, missed the boat. And I can look back and see what could have been different, but this is part of life; and this is why it is always good to listen to some older people. And if you listen, they can help us avoid certain things because they have been there, and there goes the phrase "been there, done that." I have learned that I must be in tuned with the Father through the understanding of who God is and especially who his Son, Jesus, is and the indwelling of the Holy Spirit.

I understand being confused about things, and when I am, I have learned to ask the Holy Spirit. And without the guidance of the Holy Spirit, the entire religious walk can be a lost cause because none of us can fight Satan without our helper, the Holy Spirit. I see why some people just give up. We can give up because it is truly hard to under- stand unless you have "a relationship with Jesus guided by the Holy Spirit." This relationship is a heart relationship because God/Jesus knows your heart. I find it wonderfully amazing how God works. For example, on a particular Sunday, when I had decided that when I get home from church, I would start writing again. This particular Sunday, the minister's message was entitled "It's a Heart Thing." And the definition of heart is the center of our intellect, the center of our emotions. The heart is who we are by Minister David Graham. With our hearts, we feel and believe in Jesus and accept that he is the one who lived and died for us to be connected to the Father in heaven. There is a love in our hearts and soul that words cannot explain. We try, but it is something that you just know in your heart; and when you do, there is a change in the human being that will show through to others that you are in tuned with the Father in heaven. You are still you, and you will still make mistakes and screw up; but the love for God will carry you through any situation or circumstance your life may encounter. See how God gave me a word through the minister of the day. It was for me, and I thanked God that the Holy Spirit helped me recognize it. I cannot say it enough. God is *real*. Heaven is real, and so is hell.

Another example: One morning, I was praying to God, telling him I am not worthy of this task and that I do not feel like I can do this; and in my spirit, it was as God said, "It has nothing to do with how you feel, my dear."

I want to keep it simple how to hear from God. It is the Holy Spirit in us that communicates to God for us. Some call it your consciousness, but it is the Spirit of God communicating with your spirit. And if you pay attention and listen, you can hear and know for yourself. As I am sure of the message I received and as I continue, I can tell the words are from God because of the way the words flow. I know I cannot do this on my own.

I want to continue to be who God made me to be and continue to do what God has assigned me to do. I have faith that God is using me and will help me not to doubt when the enemy tries to break me down and say to me, "Who do you think you are to take on such a task? Do you really think that something good will come from this by a simple little you?"

Scripture tells me that through Christ, I can do all things; and, to the enemy, as my mom would have said, "Satan get ye behind me, and leave me alone. I and my Father are on a journey that does not include you."

(I include little prayer and thoughts because I want the reader to know that I prayed my way through. And you can too, so whatever you have to do, you just pray your way through.)

As we mature, we try to reach other spiritual guidance which is what we depend on when talking to a person who really does not understand. I find myself telling people to pray which we all need, but we need to say more. I can remember once when I was saying, "What is the point in praying for something if it's not God's will? It shall not come to past." However, I was told we should always pray for God's will. Now that raised another question: how can I know God's will?

The answer was, when you have that right relationship with Jesus, you can find God's will. This is an area that I am still struggling with because I want to get stronger in my prayer life. As I said before, I am reaching for maturity in Christ.

Personal Prayer Story

When I learned that my mom was sick, I prayed asking God not to take my mom; but he took her. My mother was never a sickly person. She was never in the hospital during my life. In 1993, I live in Northern Virginia and was flying to Chicago for a job interview. After the interview, I contacted my sister (Ara); and she said that Mother was sick. I had talked to her the night before when I arrived, but she did not tell me about my mother's illness the night before because she did not want to upset me prior to my interview. Needless to say, a few of us got on the road and immediately headed to Arkansas. We drove all night, and I was praying all the way for her to get better.

When we arrived at the hospital and seeing my mother with tubes in her and just lying there, I begged God, "Please, do not take her now. Not now because she had gotten sick so suddenly."

I kept praying and praying asking God to heal my mother and let everything be okay. It was so hard to see my mother lying there not knowing anything. I wanted her to just open her eyes to see that I was there. I prayed so hard. I wanted to move her to another hospital if that would help, but the doctor said, "There was not much to be done." I stood there by her bed calling her name "Velma, Velma, Mother, Mom" rubbing her arm and hand but nothing. I pleaded for her to open her eyes and know I was there. I decided to go to the bathroom to pray and plead with God, "Please let her be okay."

However, a few minutes passed; and my sister came to get me because the doctors wanted to see us. At that time, they told us she was gone. At that moment, I thought my whole life would just fall apart. My best friend and confidant had passed on. I had a feeling that as if someone had taken their hands and wrapped them around my heart and squeezed it. The pain was so bad, and, at the same time, I could not breathe and needing someone to just help me. My sister held me until I was able to compose myself.

At that moment, I was angry with God for taking my mom when I had prayed and asked him not to. I told God I was angry. People had told me, "No, do not be angry with God. No, do not do that." Well, I was angry; and I said so. What I had been told by others about not getting angry with God could be words that caused a person to fall away because of their anger and thinking God does not answer prayers. Situations like this can raise another question such as "Why pray when God has it already planned?"

We do not know God's plan, but we have to keep the faith and pray. How could I have tried to keep my anger inside while trying not to be angry when God already know I was angry? I could not hide my feelings from God. He knows all, but I feel blessed for my recovery from this anger. God was already aware of and loved me despite my anger. We headed to my mother's home to start making plans for the funeral, and the sky opened up; and it rained so hard my brother could hardly see as he was driving. We finally made it to the house trying to get ourselves to comprehend what had just happened. The rain stopped, and my sister was looking out the back door; and she yelled for the other of us to come. And as we looked out the back door, there was the brightest rainbow I had ever seen. Seeing that rainbow gave me a calming feeling, and I thank God because I had to be strong enough to make decisions. With all of my pain and anger, my Father God brought me through.

If you are going through anything and you are angry with God, please, never, never, never give up on God no matter how hurt and angry you are. God knows your heart, mind, and soul. You cannot hide. Do not pretend. God knows the truth. God loves us, and with prayer, you will find peace as we realize that God knows what is best.

This is a point where I truly experience a broken heart. The pain was actually in my heart, and it hurts so bad. It is so hard to explain, but if you have been there, you know what I am saying. I was hurt so badly missing my mom. And I realized I was being selfish. I wanted my mom with me. At the same time, I know my mom's spirit was in a much better place, and as an elderly lady told me one time, "Even if the dead in Christ could come back, they would not want to." I was selfish and knew better. It took time for me to let go of the hurt. I had lost both parents within a year of each other, and I believe I was still mourning the loss of my dad; and suddenly, my mom was gone.

I thank God I was rooted in faith believing I will see my mother again. Even knowing this the hurt did not ease, it took time for this pain to ease. The pain now is not bad at all, and I can miss my mother with peace. If you lose someone you truly love, keep the faith. And pray for peace and comfort and you will make it; but remember, it takes time and faith. Allow God to be God. It will take time. This was a very hard and difficult period in my life. If it had not been for the grace of God, I could still be living in my own world of hurt and anger, but I have *joy*.

In situation of loss, time is truly our friend. If you are in a hard, difficult place, ask the Lord to lead you out of that place and, like me, learn to live the good life God has given you.

In life, so many things can happen. We can have very high highs and very low lows. I give God all the glory for both my highs and lows. No matter what your background is, keep faith in God because you never know where he will lead you. You can get angry, cry, and be disappointed; but keep going.

Finally, as I look back at life, I see God's blessings for me all over the place. When I finished college and got my first government job with the US Corp of Engineer in Little Rock, Arkansas, as a GS-5 making a little over six thousand dollars a year, I knew I had made it. Little did I know what God had a head for me. Because of my upbringing as I previously stated, I always found a church to attend for worship to be with other believers no matter where I moved.

I left Little Rock, Arkansas, with a promotion and moved to Fort Worth, Texas. And while being there, I found a local church. And this is where I heard an encouraging passage quoted each week by my then pastor that has stayed with me, and it is from Isaiah 40:28–31 (KJV) that reads as follows:

> Hast thou not known? Hast thou not heard,
> that the everlasting God, the Lord, the Creator

> of the ends of the earth, fainteth not, neither is weary? There is no searching of his understand.
>
> He giveth power to the faint; and to them that have no might he increases strength.
>
> Even the youths shall faint and be weary, and the young men shall utterly fall:
>
> But they that wait upon the Lord shall renew their strength; they shall mount up with wings as eagles; they shall run, and not be weary; and they shall walk, and not faint.

This was so powerful that I quoted it for years believing each word. I can witness to others how then I had no idea what was going on and felt angry and hurt but always prayed and kept the faith, and it was so hard at times. While living in Fort Worth, I married and divorced. This was one of the lows, a very difficult time. But with prayer, God brought me through. This could be a story in itself. I must say I know who brought me out of this bad situation. My God is always taking care of me.

With the normal progression, I moved to the Chicago area as a GS-11 auditor and soon received my promotion to a GS-12. I remember asking God at this point to allow me to retire early; and, at the time, I believe I was in my late thirties thinking about retiring. This is to show you how God can work in your life. I worked for the federal government my entire professional career, and I finished my career working in Washington, DC, and I will not go into details. I believed I had to file an Equal Employment Opportunity Commission (EEOC) Complaint because I believed I had been targeted as a troublemaker and was discriminated against. I could not see myself just going with the flow regardless if it was right or wrong without ethics. I praise God for the support of my local church.

However, once I filed that complaint, I became an enemy of the organization. I would do work with others; and the other persons would get recognition and rewarded. And my name would be left off as if I had done nothing even if most of the work would have my confirmation on it. I was given assignment designed to fail and criticized for every effort or project. As with any story, there are always two sides, and I can only tell mine.

However, during this time, I felt like I was a target; and arrows were coming from all directions. This was a time when being covered everyday with the Armor of God was such a blessing as described in the scriptures below.

The Armor of God

> Finally, be strong in the Lord and in his mighty power. Put on the full armor of God, so that you can take your stand against the devil's schemes. For our struggle is not against flesh and blood, but against the rulers, against the authorities, against the powers of this dark world and against the spiritual forces of evil in the heavenly realms. Therefore put on the full armor of God, so that when the day of evil comes, you may be able to stand your ground, and after you have done everything, to stand. Stand firm then, with the belt of truth buckled around your waist, with the breastplate of righteousness in place, and with your feet fitted with the readiness that comes from the gospel of peace. In addition to all this, take up the shield of faith, with which you can extinguish all the flaming arrows of the evil one. Take the helmet of salvation and the sword of the Spirit, which is the word of God.
>
> And pray in the Spirit on all occasions with all kinds of prayers and requests. With this in mind, be alert and always keep on praying for all the Lord's people.

I had several years of hardship. I cried and prayed and believe that God was with me, but it was an awful time in my life. I had prayed and prayed, and God brought me through. But at times, I was thinking God had forgotten me or just did not hear me. I never, never, stopped believing and praying. God does answer prayers not as we may imagine because God works at his own pace. And for those who love the Lord, in hindsight, I know that God's timing and plan is the best. I understand now because of my choices and decisions to file the complaint, may have caused this hardship and difficult time because I did not put my total trust in God and being the best Christian employee possible and respect whom God had placed in authority over me. I believe I could have avoided some or all of the difficulties but even with my messing up of things, God made a way; it worked out for the good.

In hindsight, I can see that because of my decision to file a complaint, I caused all this difficulty on myself because I did not trust totally in God by being the best Christian employee as possible with respect for whom God had placed in authority over me. I cannot say with certainty that my situation would have changed because sometimes, hardship is the way that God teaches us things.

With all that had happened and with situations looking bad, I won my case; and my legal expenses were reimbursed, and I was rewarded by being able to retire at the age of fifty-two with benefits but a 10 percent cut in my retirement pay. With my messing up with things my way, God did work it out for the good. Hear me please when I was at the negotiation table and found out that I had won, I cried and I cried because at the time, I wanted the promotion I was fighting for and to finish my last three years. Now a few days after asking God "why me, why couldn't I have gotten the promotion," and like a brick, it hits me. God reminded me, "You asked me to allow you to retire early."

I had to laugh at myself and apologize to God and thank the Holy Spirit for bringing to my remembrance what I had asked for, and God had answered my prayer I prayed years ago. I wasn't fired. I did not have to quit. I retired, hallelujah! When he answers prayers, he does not tell us how or when, and like me, we can believe God has forgotten all about you. But in his timing, your blessing can be right around the corner. With everything I went through, I became a much stronger person; and I truly learned to have more patience.

We do not know what lessons there are for us to learn. So when you are going through something no matter how bad, do not give up on God. He is always on your side. You may not see it or feel it, but keep on pushing forward. You may feel that he has left you; but if he has ever been with you, he will never leave you. In everything I have read in the Bible, never did I see in his Word that if we follow Jesus and believe on Jesus, life would be easy. I can see God was always with me. If Jesus had it hard and we are heirs, then what can we expect? God did not say our life journey would be easy.

Fellow believers and nonbelievers alike, Jesus is the way to heaven. Heaven is our hope. Paul said that to be absent from the body is to be present with the Lord. What better hope can we have than that? The Bible also tells us what to expect. Remember, we never grow up but keep your eyes on the prize—the new body. In 2 Corinthians 5:1–7 NIV, it says:

> For we know that if the earthly tent we live in is destroyed, we have a building from God, an eternal house in heaven, not build by human hands. Meanwhile we groan, longing to be clothed instead with our heavenly dwelling because when we are clothed, we will not be found naked. For while we are in this tent, we groan and are burdened, because we do not wish to be unclothed but to be clothed instead with our heavenly dwelling, so that what is mortal may be swallowed up by life. Now the one who has fashioned us for this very purpose is God, who has given us the Spirit as a deposit, guaranteeing what is to come. Therefore we are always confident and know that as long as we are at home in the body we are away from the Lord. For we live by faith, not by sight.

Prayer

Prayer is very important, and this is one of the areas where I am always comparing, and God tells me to stop. I believe in prayer. I pray, and I know God answers prayers, but prayer is not a magic wand that each prayer we pray has the answer yes, and I used to be so disappointed and think that God just doesn't answer my prayers; but I learned over the years how it works because one prayer can be with a wrong motive and wrong idea, but scriptures teach us about prayer.

James 4:3 (NIV) teaches us that "When you ask, you do not receive, because you ask with wrong motives, that you may spend what you get on your pleasures," and Luke 18:1 (NIV) states: "Then Jesus told his disciples a parable to show them that they should always pray and not give up."

And Ephesians 6:18 (NIV) says: "And pray in the Spirit on all occasions with all kinds of prayers and request. With this in mind, be alert and always keep on praying for all the Lord's people."

As I conclude, I pray that something has been or will be said to help someone with just a little bit of understanding how great/complex and loving Christianity is with the endless love our Savior, Jesus Christ.

Conclusion

I ask, "Where are you? And where do you want to be?"

As for me, I know I am saved; and I am a child of God, an heir. This is where I am, yet there is so much more. I am reaching for maturity where every inch of me is depending solely on my Lord and Savior for everything.

Through life, I see simplicity and complexity in everything we do depending on the person and God's guidance and gifts he has given each of us. Some people can make simple complex, and others can make complex simple. As I ponder over God telling me over and over not to compare myself to others; just maybe, after all these years, I finally got it. I am to use the gifts God has given me to live the life he has given me to his glory and just leave the rest to him.

I have learned to not block my blessings while trying to prophesize when that is not my gift. Our Father asks to put your focus on him and asks to know your gift, and he will show you. Love the lord with all your heart and soul. We are not perfect, and we are all sinners; but by his grace and love, we can live the life he has given us to his glory.

Please, please do not condemn yourself like I did, comparing or wishing for what you do not have, for God has already given you all you need to seek his face and be Christlike and "not Christ." Be Christlike, and live the life he has for you to his glory being heaven-bound. I will keep learning until the day I transition to the other side with my Jesus.

Finally, I want to thank the Lord above for giving me this task and the guidance to do it. If it goes no further than the pages I have written it on, I say thank you, Father, for using me to teach me. Father God, when I reread what has been written in some areas, I can

Prayer

Prayer is very important, and this is one of the areas where I am always comparing, and God tells me to stop. I believe in prayer. I pray, and I know God answers prayers, but prayer is not a magic wand that each prayer we pray has the answer yes, and I used to be so disappointed and think that God just doesn't answer my prayers; but I learned over the years how it works because one prayer can be with a wrong motive and wrong idea, but scriptures teach us about prayer.

James 4:3 (NIV) teaches us that "When you ask, you do not receive, because you ask with wrong motives, that you may spend what you get on your pleasures," and Luke 18:1 (NIV) states: "Then Jesus told his disciples a parable to show them that they should always pray and not give up."

And Ephesians 6:18 (NIV) says: "And pray in the Spirit on all occasions with all kinds of prayers and request. With this in mind, be alert and always keep on praying for all the Lord's people."

As I conclude, I pray that something has been or will be said to help someone with just a little bit of understanding how great/complex and loving Christianity is with the endless love our Savior, Jesus Christ.

Conclusion

I ask, "Where are you? And where do you want to be?"

As for me, I know I am saved; and I am a child of God, an heir. This is where I am, yet there is so much more. I am reaching for maturity where every inch of me is depending solely on my Lord and Savior for everything.

Through life, I see simplicity and complexity in everything we do depending on the person and God's guidance and gifts he has given each of us. Some people can make simple complex, and others can make complex simple. As I ponder over God telling me over and over not to compare myself to others; just maybe, after all these years, I finally got it. I am to use the gifts God has given me to live the life he has given me to his glory and just leave the rest to him.

I have learned to not block my blessings while trying to prophesize when that is not my gift. Our Father asks to put your focus on him and asks to know your gift, and he will show you. Love the lord with all your heart and soul. We are not perfect, and we are all sinners; but by his grace and love, we can live the life he has given us to his glory.

Please, please do not condemn yourself like I did, comparing or wishing for what you do not have, for God has already given you all you need to seek his face and be Christlike and "not Christ." Be Christlike, and live the life he has for you to his glory being heaven-bound. I will keep learning until the day I transition to the other side with my Jesus.

Finally, I want to thank the Lord above for giving me this task and the guidance to do it. If it goes no further than the pages I have written it on, I say thank you, Father, for using me to teach me. Father God, when I reread what has been written in some areas, I can see where the Holy Spirit had the pen because there is no way could that have come from me.

As for my goal, I do pray to God asking that this story will help someone with their spiritual growth for which I have truly learned the "Then what?" (Spiritual Growth)

Thank you, Jesus, with all my heart. Amen.

Reference

Eugene H. Peterson. *The Message (MSG)*. 1993,1994,199–2002.
Gateway Bible (Gatewaybible.com)
Hasting dictionary of the Bible, Hendrickson Published, Inc. edition reprinted from the edition originally Published by Charles Scribner's Sons New York, 1909
King James Version (KJV) Public Domain
New Living Translation (NTL) Holy Bible. New Living Translation. Tyndale House Foundation, 1996,2004,2015.
New Revised Standard Version (NRSV). United States of America: Division of Christian Education of the National Council of the Churches of Christ, 1989.
Third College Edition Webster's New World Dictionary of American English copyright 1988 by Simon & Schuster, Inc
The Living Bible (TLB). Tyndale House Foundation, 1971.
The Lockman Foundation. New American Standard Bible (NASB), 1960,1962,1963–1995.

About the Author

Vervely Jordan grew up in a tiny little place called Lakeview, Arkansas. She is a graduate of the University of Arkansas, Pine Bluff, with an accounting degree. She retired from the federal government after a little over thirty years with at least twenty-five years as an auditor for the United States Department of Energy, Office of Inspector General, in Washington DC. She currently volunteers as a bookkeeper locally and attends church at Rejoice Church in Olive Branch, Mississippi, where she and her husband, Garry Williams, reside.